BREAKING SILENCE

A CLOSE LOOK AT DIVORCE, REMARRIAGE, AND ABUSE

DESTINE REID

WESTBOW
PRESS
A DIVISION OF THOMAS NELSON

WestBow Press books may be ordered through booksellers or by contacting:

WestBow Press
A Division of Thomas Nelson
1663 Liberty Drive
Bloomington, IN 47403
www.westbowpress.com
1 (866) 928-1240

ISBN: 978-1-4908-1039-3 (sc)

Library of Congress Control Number: 2013917778

Printed in the United States of America.

WestBow Press rev. date: 10/22/2013

CONTENTS

DEDICATION

This book is dedicated to my wonderful parents, Carlton and Anetta Blair, who have been married for thirty five years now. I am so very grateful that God in all His love and wisdom saw it fit to give me parents like you. You have been and continue to be a great blessing and inspiration to me. I especially want to give all glory, honor and thanksgiving to God for healing and blessing my mom with life after a recent heart attack. This demonstration of His power and love has given us all a new lease on life. Thank you both for your continuous love, support and prayers. I love you always.

ACKNOWLEDGEMENT

Above all, I give praise, glory and honor to the Most High God my heavenly Father whose enabling power led to the completion of the first of my inspirational pennings. This serves as a testimony that He who began a good work in us is faithful to complete it. I testify of the spiritual revelation to which I was exposed via His word and truly appreciate the constant renewal of the mind that occurs as a result of seeking after truth.

I express heartfelt thanks to my darling husband, Albert, for his unending support even as I tap into the gift God has deposited in me. Sweetheart, there is nothing more rewarding than gaining the confidence of our loved ones; especially when you decide to journey in unfamiliar territories. I value your input and love you very much.

Also, to our daughter Destiny whose constant enquiry as to my progress in the process of penning served as a means of provoking me to finish what I started. You were truly a source of motivation and I really am blessed.

High to commendation is duly extended to Pastor Miladys Thomas whose guidance in the area of Christian counseling served to unlock a new dimension of ministry in me. Your sacrifice and encouragement certainly did not go unnoticed for you made learning practical and life changing.

As human beings we cannot ignore tangible acts of love; especially when they come from a sister, friend and covenant partner—Minister Maylene Christiani. I want to express profound gratitude to you for your prayers as well as words of encouragement which hinged directly on pursing the deep things of the Spirit. Your affirmation surely served me well.

Honor is in line for Apostle Gerald and Pastor Elsa Lafleur whose apostolic covering and spiritual guidance provided a platform for the demonstration of the gifts in me. Your words of wisdom have borne much fruit in my life and will definitely serve to refresh many others in the secular domain as well as those in the kingdom of God.

Thank you Lord for the community of women at Restoration Ministries to which you have aligned me so we could labor together. They have contributed to the enrichment of my life by investing their time, talent and treasure and I found it quite enabling. Ladies, your sisterly gestures have quantum leaped my spiritual maturity and I find refinement in your company.

God in His wisdom paved the way for a divine connection with the editor, Mrs. Claudette Paul who devoted her time to ensuring that my passion for sharing the heart of God with the rest of the world becomes a reality. May God reward you richly.

Finally, I thank all those who read this book and pray that you would be willing to embrace the truths found within and as a result you will become enriched even as you seek to act upon God's instructions; under the influence of the Holy Spirit.

INTRODUCTION

Marriage and family have been instituted by God and are the foundations of the church, communities, and nations. Modern thinking/views have dented significant blows to marriages and family life to the point where the divorce rates have increased astronomically. The purpose of this book is to take a closer look at divorce, remarriage and various forms of abuse (such as physical, emotional, verbal) and to identify how they affect the individual, marriages, and the family unit. Moreover, I shall examine the word of God for His position on it all.

For years, many Christians have raised questions concerning the act of divorce: is it a sin? On what grounds should the same be pursued? Can a person who is divorced get married to someone else? How does the word of God speak to the issue of divorce? This, in particular, is a much debated and highly inflammable subject in the Christian community.

There are so many opinions, views, doctrines, revelations, interpretations, misinterpretations which have influenced the church's view on this subject of divorce and have left a greater percentage of the persons in uncertainty, primarily, those who are faced with the difficult decision of divorcing a spouse and marrying another. In addressing these questions and in speaking to the general population, both of Christians and non-Christians, we will encounter numerous philosophical and theological points of view. Previously, some of the very questions were posited to me but due to insufficient knowledge of the truth; I either shied away or refused to comment. I got married at the age of twenty three and in the midst of marital challenges; I must confess that I have contemplated divorce on numerous occasions. Naturally, I wanted to establish whether I would be able to remarry and if so under what circumstances. Now looking back, I realize that at that point of my life I was actually afraid that if I inquired of the Lord on this matter I would not have liked the answer He would have given. So despite of my love and hot pursuit after His heart and mind, these issues I somewhat failed to inquire about. A few months ago while taking a course in Christian Counseling, I was instructed by my teacher to conduct a study and write a paper on divorce, remarriage and abuse. I had such a mental block to these issues, particularly, divorce that I procrastinated for months before starting my assignment. As I studied, God started dealing with me by revealing my stubbornness to promote my desires above His will. As His Spirit taught me His mind and heart for marriage and family, my mind, life and marriage were being set on the path of transformation. I came to realize that refusal to accept the word of God keeps me from the truth that can set me free.

Our decisions must be based on the truth i.e. the word of God which outlines His will, thoughts and desires, for His people. God's word sets the standard for our lives and, therefore, must be immediately consulted in moments of doubt, uncertainty or skepticism. In Psalms 138:2, we see that God magnifies His word above His very name. It means that He has placed a high value on His word. By His word (His counsel, His decree) worlds were made. Therefore, we need to view and value God's word for what it is: His full council. The only way we can arrive at the correct position on the issues of divorce, remarriage and abuse is by consulting His word.

You may be seeking understanding concerning divorce, remarriage, abuse, and how to overcome them. It is not by accident that you are currently reading this book which is an attempt to answer certain related questions. It does not address every detail pertaining to the topics presented; for according to John 21:25, even the Bible in all its precision and universality does not encapsulate all that transpired historically. I pray, however, that you may find information and insight that would further enrich, exhort, encourage and edify you in your relations and would help to propel you further into your divine destiny.

PART 1
DIVORCE AND REMARRIAGE

CHAPTER ONE

WHAT IS MARRIAGE?

"God created marriage. No government subcommittee envisioned it. No social organization developed it. Marriage was conceived and born in the mind of God." **Max Lucado**

Marriage has its origin deep in history; as far back as the creation of mankind. Nelson's Bible dictionary defines it as "the union between a man and a woman as husband and wife, which becomes the foundation of a home and family". It is the uniting of a man and his wife; the joining of two individuals not only physically but mentally and spiritually and was ordained by God to be a covenant, a binding agreement, which is contrary to a contract which is an agreement for a specified period of time.

In the Genesis' account, we see that God created everything and He said/saw each was good:

- He created light and **saw** that it was good (Gen 1:3).
- He created land and sea and **saw** it was good. (Gen1:9,10)
- He created vegetation and **saw** it was good. (Gen 1:11,12)
- He created sun, moon and stars and saw it was **good**. (Gen1:14-16)
- He created birds of all sorts and **saw** it was good. (Gen 1:20-21)
- He created the animals and **saw** it was good. (Gen 1:24,25)

Then He looked at man living in the garden where He had placed him; doing the job He placed him there to do; with enough resources to sustain him yet he was operating alone and He declared it is not good for man to be alone.

> *And the Lord God said, It is not good that the man*
> *should be alone; I will make him an help meet for him.*

Gen 2:18

Here we see God made a twofold statement:

1. "... it is not good that the man should be alone" (the point of concern)
2. "... I will make him an help meet for him" (the solution)

God then proceeded to make animals:

> *19 And out of the ground the Lord God formed every beast*
> *of the field, and every fowl of the air; and brought them unto*
> *Adam to see what he would call them: and whatsoever Adam*
> *called every living creature, that was the name thereof.*
>
> *20 And Adam gave names to all cattle, and to the fowl*
> *of the air, and to every beast of the field; but for Adam*
> ***there was not found an help meet for him.***

Gen 2:19-20

Even after God had made the birds and animals, there was no help meet found for man. They served as mere companions for him but not a help meet which fit God's intent for him. So, why is it that so many persons think they could replace their spouses or marriage with money, friends, and careers?

The answer to man's loneliness was God's provision of a help meet for him. Who, therefore, is a help meet? It actually means a help suitable for him; she who would assist him in executing God's mandate for his life.

Thus, her role is a very important one. For the sake of argument many may seek to question: are all women help meets? Well that's an entirely different subject which will certainly be addressed in future pennings.

4

We can see from the very beginning that in the mind of God marriage was and is good. In Genesis 1:31, He declared that everything He made including the union of the man and woman was very good. Let me bring clarity to one word at this point. As you would have observed, I emphasized "saw". The word "saw" is derived from the Hebrew word ra'ah which is "to see" and has included in its meaning "to approve. While the word good is defined as being healthy, beneficial, profitable, advantageous, useful, commendable, excellent, rightful and satisfactory. Interestingly enough, the word "that" actually means the same as certainly, rightly, without a doubt. So the text actually reads ". . . . and God saw (approved) that (certainly, rightly, without a doubt) good". In other words, God approved without a doubt that all He had made including the marriage between man and woman was healthy, beneficial, excellent and profitable.

Marriage according to God's order should meet the needs of both—parties (man and woman). Now, I know such a statement would raise eyebrows in the secular world as well as in the church, primarily because we are living in a world where humanism[1] teaches us that we create and steer our own destinies, and that we are self reliant, self sufficient, self fulfilled, and therefore need no one; not even God. Over the years we have seen conformity to such philosophies and doctrines in the church and they are totally contrary to God's original plan for mankind.

According to our modern criteria for success, we would say Adam had it made.

15 And the Lord God took the man, and put him into the garden of Eden to dress it and to keep it.

16 And the Lord God commanded the man, saying, Of every tree of the garden thou mayest freely eat:

---

[1] **Humanism** - A system of thought that rejects religious beliefs and centers on humans and their values, capacities, and worth.

17 But of the tree of the knowledge of good and
evil, thou shalt not eat of it: for in the day that
thou eatest thereof thou shalt surely die.

18 And the Lord God said, It is not good that the man
should be alone; I will make him an help meet for him.

19 And out of the ground the Lord God formed every beast
of the field and every fowl of the air; and brought them unto
Adam to see what he would call them: and whatsoever Adam
called every living creature that was the name thereof.

20 And Adam gave names to all cattle, and to the
fowl of the air and to every beast of the field; but for
Adam there was not found a help meet for him.

Gen 2:15-20

Our perception of success differs greatly from God's so we tend to judge a person and make many decisions based on how we feel or what we see with the naked eye. We would save ourselves from a lot of heartache if we just inquire of God by seeking counsel from His word before getting involved in certain relationships or making certain commitments. I am reminded of the prophet Samuel who went to the house of Jesse to anoint the next king of Israel. When Eliab, one of Jesse's sons walked in, Samuel looked at him and thought "this must be God's anointed king". God had to interject and admonish Samuel not to look at the physical appearance or stature. Rather, He—God looks at the heart. Remember Saul had looked like a king based on man's criteria but his heart was far from God; for he was stubborn and rebellious. Although David was the youngest, very ruddy in appearance, dwelt among and smelled of sheep, he was chosen! I imagine he was the kind of person that most of us would have held our breath in anticipation of his scent if he was to walk by but God saw his heart and he grew to become "a man after God's own heart". For he, David, possessed the heart of a worshipper. Yes, he made mistakes but he listened to counsel, accepted rebuke, acknowledged his wrongs and truly repented. We cannot determine a person's true success and their worth by how they look. We cannot disqualify a person from the purposes of God because of his or her past, their jobs nor their education.

The Importance of Right Connection

How often have we been hooked up in the wrong relationship, formed ungodly alliances; made ill informed business decisions and entered into unequally yoked marriages? The right connections are needed if we are going to accomplish what God has for us; especially when we consider where God is taking the church. In Amos 3:3, the question is asked *"Can two walk together, unless they are agreed?"* (NKJV): for there to be advancement, there must be agreement. Think of it as a three legged race: the persons are joined together and unless they both agree to go in the same direction they will both fall and most likely get hurt. Agreement speaks of being in sync or in harmony with one another at the point where we speak the same language, and are in one accord. Although each person is different, common focus, similarity in values, motives, and principles make them one. This was exactly the atmosphere on the day of Pentecost as outlined in Acts 2:1-2.

> *When the Day of Pentecost had fully come, they were all with one accord in one place. 2 And suddenly there came a sound from heaven, as of a rushing mighty wind, and it filled the whole house where they were sitting.*

Acts 2:1-3

The scripture says that they were in *one* accord in *one* place. It means that they were in agreement; having the same desire, focus and expectation. This captured heaven's attention and the Godhead promptly responded by filling them to the overflow; in that those who heard the noise were drawn to where they were. Our agreement here on earth whether in relationships, marriage, business, church, will unlock new dimensions to us and summon heaven's response.

> *19 "Again, I tell you that if two of you on earth*
> *agree about anything you ask for, it will be*
> *done for you by my Father in heaven.*

Matt 18:19-20

Our decisions concerning the relationships we form must not be taken lightly and therefore cannot be determined solely on external factors. Note my position that the relationships cannot be based solely on those factor but they should be taken into consideration. For example, Adam had a job, a home, a mandate and therefore knew where he was going before a wife was added to him. There are too many persons getting married solely on the basis of emotional fantasies. In some instances, the man has no job, no idea where they are going to live, emotional baggage and a passion for marriage.

Marriage is Good

If Adam were in today's society, he would be considered a very successful man: he was living in the garden which meant he had a home; he was taking care of garden including the animals which meant he had a job; he had the animals as his companions and that meant he had friends. In fact, the Bible says God would come and commune with him. This means he had a relationship with God. Yet, God declared it was not *good* for him to be alone. Why would God say such a thing? Isn't that what marriage is about? Isn't it all about companionship, financial stability and security? All of these are questions you may be asking and yes they may be benefits of marriage. Many persons think that if a person has a house, car, good job, food, and friends; they have reached the pinnacle of their achievements. However, since God said that it is not good, it is a clear indication that His purpose, thoughts and intent for marriage extends beyond the acquisition of the aforementioned things.

Now, let us examine the intent for marriage. I have heard persons ask, "What is the use of having a man or woman when I can accomplish much on my own? What can he or she add to my life? The reasoning is that marriage just adds stress to one's life and happiness is better achieved without having to join one's self to a husband or wife. Every day we hear of husbands and wives choosing their jobs, another person, money, friends over their marriages all in pursuit of happiness and fulfilling their idea of true purpose in life. They are convinced that they can fulfill their purpose on their own.

Admittedly, there are persons, who do not get married but their motive for doing so is not selfish. As you will see later that marriage is not intended for everyone; as in the case of the Apostle Paul. However, even in such cases, these single people are expected to commit themselves to some form of relationship for we all need someone. Wholesome relationships are not easily mastered but they are absolutely necessary if we are going to be successful in life. The truth is that the 'lone ranger' mentality reflects a misconception of the true purpose of marriage and the need for partnership, for even the Lone Ranger needed Tonto.

If we are able to apprehend the true purpose of marriage, we will be better positioned to walk in it and reap the full benefits. Think about it; if you do not know what you are looking for, how will you recognize it when you see it? God saying that it is not good for man to be alone is a clear indication that His purpose, thoughts, intent for marriage extends beyond satisfying of fleshly desires which we will look more in depth at as we continue.

When God joined the man and his wife their mandate was clearly communicated, defined and understood by them both. We must ask ourselves, husbands, wives and intended—where is our marriage going? Marriage must have a focus. It is when we lose focus and break the rules of engagement for the marriage that the purpose is derailed and chaos steps in like we saw in the case of Adam and Eve. The purpose of the marriage must be clearly defined, communicated, understood and adhered to by both parties. God as the initiator of marriage has outlined in His word, His will and desires for it. I want to reiterate that it is in the best interest of the relationship to seek His counsel if our marriages are going to be truly successful.

Chapter Highlights

- Marriage was ordained by God to be a covenant not a contract
- The solution to the loneliness of the man is a help meet
- Marriage according to God's order is beneficial and needful to both parties.
- Wholesome relationships are not easily maintained but they are absolutely necessary if we are going to be successful in life.
- The purpose of the marriage must be clearly defined, communicated, understood and adhered to by both parties.

CHAPTER TWO

DOUBLE IMPACT

"Sex appeal alone is the poorest basis in the world for a happy marriage." **John R. Rice**

Jeremy and Janice (whose names have been changed) were saved for many years and had been married for almost thirteen years. For the first eleven years, it seemed like their marriage was going around in circles. They constantly argued, fought, got involved in affairs and separated on numerous occasions. They kept wondering if they had made the right decision to be united in marriage and if it was God's will for them. No one gave their all to the marriage because they were unsure of its reward. It seemed like God was silent and both of them kept seeking excuses to leave. Eventually, Janice decided that she had endured enough and was adamant on filing for a divorce irrespective of what anyone said because she felt the marriage was a waste of time. Then one evening, a minister of the gospel visited them with a word from God. He spoke many things to them but what stood out most was this revelation: "the purpose of this marriage has never been defined".

Identifying the Purpose of Marriage

Before an invention materializes, its purpose is already in the mind of its inventor. Purpose gives definition to the creation. Likewise, it is very important for the marriage to be defined if success is to be achieved. After looking at Genesis' account of the union between man and woman, we see that the purpose for marriage is much more than jobs, cars, money and legal sex. Before God instituted marriage He had a great purpose in mind for the union. Sadly however, too often we do not take time to inquire of God since we somehow assume that we know the reason why we get married. It is not by accident that God joined the man and woman together. Each gender is different from the other, but the differences are actually the strength of the relationship and if each understands and embraces the other for who God has created him/her to be, it makes for greater functionality.

Let me explain: women are generally the more perceptive of the two while men generally assume an executive role. If each is functioning in his or her God-ordained capacity, they will automatically become an absolutely effective team. They form the government of the family and its foundation. This structure for marriage and the family is similar to that of the church which according to Ephesians 2:20 is built on the foundation of the Apostles (the executive arm) and Prophets (Inspiration and perception) with Christ being the chief cornerstone. Both the husband and wife need to understand and appreciate the individual God has created them to be if they are going to function in their correct capacity yet remain a team. Man, you need for your wife to understand and embrace the individual God has created and called her to be if she is going to benefit the marriage while the woman needs for her husband to understand and embrace the individual God has created and called him to be if he is going to benefit the marriage. Do not frustrate each others' purpose! It is not accidental that women are more thinkers while men are more likely to act. Can you image all actions without anyone thinking? I am of the form conviction that it was a deliberate act on the part of the Creator to put the man and woman together; since their individual attributes become necessary to complete a task and to fulfill His mandate.

Passion versus Purpose

It can be very troubling when persons in the Christian community choose 'shotgun marriage' which only occurs on the condition where fornication resulted in pregnancy. Marriages based on these reasons have often been disastrous and very often do not last. Many leaders have also defended this rationale with the Apostle Paul's statement in 1 Corinthians 7:9:

> *But if they have not self-control (restraint of their passions), they should marry. For it is better to marry than to be aflame *(**burn**) [with passion and tortured continually with ungratified desire].*

There are many who get married because they simply do not want to burn with passion. This is a reflection of the lack of self control and more often than not, the problem that follows is that although many marry to avoid the sin of fornication, there are still many people who are burning with desire within their marriages and still end up getting involved in sexual immorality. We will explore this in much more detail at a later time. So this brings us back to our questions: why should we get married and what was God's rationale for designing marriage?

Some months ago, I was invited to speak to a group of young people on the subject of dating, sex and relationship. During the session, one of the young women pointed out that the church is lacking Christian men of a certain calibre for women to marry and that she did not see anything wrong with a Christian woman marrying a good unsaved man. She further highlighted the fact that there are many non-Christian men and women who display more righteousness attributes than those in the church. Well, you can imagine my plight since many would agree with her statement. In truth, an ungodly man/woman or a non-Christian cannot be more righteous because righteousness speaks of right relationship/

fellowship with God and He has no fellowship with darkness (1John 1:6). I believe she was actually referring to the lifestyles since, sadly, many 'Christians/church goers' engage in some sinful practices while they continue to minister to the people of God. On the other hand, some non-Christians are afraid to enter the church building because they are conscious of their involvement in ungodly practices.

By this time, all eyes were on my assistant and I as the group eagerly awaited our response. We attempted to give the usual learnt response outlined in 2 Corinthians 6:14 and Amos 3:3: of "be not unequally yoked with unbelievers", and "two cannot walk unless they agree". These are all very true and must be followed if we are going to save ourselves from the disastrous repercussions of wrong alliances. But to these young people these were just empty, rehearsed sentences. Just then the Holy Spirit brought a passage of scripture to my mind which would strengthen and greatly explain the importance of agreement in marriage (being equally yoked).

> *And did not God make [you and your wife] one [flesh]?*
> *Did not One make you and preserve your spirit alive?*
> *And why [did God make you two] one?* **Because**
> **He sought a godly offspring [from your union].**
> *Therefore take heed to yourselves, and let no one deal*
> *treacherously and be faithless to the wife of his youth.*
>
> **Mal 2:15** (my emphasis)

Malachi said the reason God made the two become one, was for them to bring forth out of their marriage a godly offspring. At first glance this may appear to make no sense but let's look at it closely.

When God created them back in the Garden of Eden, He issued a command to them both:

> *So God created man in His own image; in the image of*
> *God He created him; male and female He created them.*

> *28 Then God blessed them, and God said to them, "Be fruitful and multiply; fill the earth and subdue it; have dominion over the fish of the sea, over the birds of the air, and over every living thing that moves on the earth."*

Gen 1:27-28

The words *'fruitful'*, *'multiply'*, *'replenish'* (fill) all entail the concept of increase. The man and woman, husband and wife, were expected to reproduce; not just in terms of having children but after their kind. That means that the godly should produce godly. The same way God breathed or exhaled life into man when He made him in His image and likeness. Man in turn is to breathe or exhale life into his offspring through his teaching and transferal of the principles of God's word into them thus transforming them into his (man's) image and likeness which was and is already supposed to be God's image and likeness. When this happens, we experience what I call a domino effect of godliness from one generation to another. In this way, the systems of this world are being demolished while the kingdom of God is being expanded.

A godly spouse covenanted to an ungodly spouse would have conflicting beliefs and values which is likely to result in a child with mixed values. The resultant factor is double-mindedness and instability in all his ways. If we fully understand the purpose for marriage, our approach to it would be totally different for our marriages are intended to glorify God.

Although God has outlined in His word the reason for marriage, individuals usually have a number of reasons why they choose to get married and to whom they choose to marry. Their reasons may range from looks to finance, or religious and cultural beliefs. These reasons greatly affect the outcome of the marriage. For example, a young man marrying his wife because she has an hour glass figure may eventually lose interest when they have had three children and the hour glass has now become a jute box. When their reason for marrying is gone many seek a way of getting out of the marriage so they could continue pursuing their ideal. Many marriages are ending in divorce because the marriage was entered into with the wrong motive.

Chapter Highlights

- Purpose gives definition to creation.
- The differences between the genders are actually the strength of the relationship
- Both the husband and wife must understand and function in their God-ordained capacity.
- Putting the man and woman together was a deliberate act by the Creator since their individual attributes are needed to complete assigned task and to fulfill their God-given mandate.
- Since man was created in the image and likeness of God, he is expected to transfer the same to his offspring. This is done through teaching and transferal of the principles of God's word.

CHAPTER THREE

DIVORCE: THE COVENANT BREAKER

"When people get married because they think it's a long-time love affair, they'll be divorced very soon, because all love affairs end in disappointment. But marriage is recognition of a spiritual identity." ~ **Joseph Campbell**

[i]Divorce can be defined as the final termination of marital union cancelling legal duties and responsibilities of marriage and dissolving the bonds of the marriage matrimony. In Malachi 2:16, God voiced His disapproval of it:

> *6 For the Lord, the God of Israel, says: I hate divorce and marital separation and him who covers his garment [his wife] with violence.*

> **Mal 2:16**

The New Living Translation says:

> *"For I hate divorce!" says the Lord, the God of Israel. "To divorce your wife is to overwhelm her with cruelty," says the Lord of Heaven's Armies. "So guard your heart; do not be unfaithful to your wife."*

> **Mal 2:16**

Imagine these are words uttered by God Himself yet there are so many divorces particularly in the Body of Christ? It is a perversion[2] of the marriage institution which He ordained for His glory. [ii]The marriage relationship was to complement the union of the man and wife and was to be a reflection of the relationship of the God Head and service to God.

Divorce can be dated back thousands of years to the Mosaic times. [iii]It was first mentioned in the Mosaic covenant (Lev. 21:14; Deut. 22:13-19; 22:28-29) but was already occurring in Israel. This was a growing problem in Israel and was done for all types of frivolous and unjustifiable reasons. In today's world, it is believed that if we are to use the divorce statistics in the church as an indication of where marriages are going; we would conclude that marriage may not survive the next two decades. This is a very ugly reflection of disloyalty and unfaithfulness staring back at us. The divorce rate in the church is currently competing very closely with that of the world and is a cause for concern. This would cause the onlooker to conclude that the minds of those in the church are more or less the same as those in the world. Where then is the transformation by the renewing of our minds which Paul pleaded for in Romans 12:2?

> *Do not be conformed to this world (this age), [fashioned after and adapted to its external, superficial customs], but be transformed (changed) by the [entire] renewal of your mind [by its new ideals and its new attitude], so that you may prove [for yourselves] what is the good and acceptable and perfect will of God, even the thing which is good and acceptable and perfect [in His sight for you].*

Rom 12:2

---

[2] PERVERSION - **turning of good into bad:** the changing of something good, true, or correct into something bad or wrong, or a situation in which the change has occurred

In order for us to truly understand what divorce is and what it does, we must first understand what marriage is. To marry means to tie, to string, to strap, to stitch, **to knit**, to chain, lock, pin, nail, bolt, clasp, crimp, **screw**, **solder**, set, **weld together**, **fuse together**, wedge, **absorb**, **melt into one**, and **to cement a union**. Just picture it for a moment, two entities which are welded together or melted into each other; no longer separate but ONE. With such a riveting imagery in mind, we can see that the two once married to each other cannot be easily separated. These words defining marriage, particularly those emphasized, scream SEAMLESSNESS. It therefore means that separating this seamless union cannot occur without one or both parties being damaged in the process. Looking at many divorcees externally and the constant rising divorce rate, we could easily assume that getting a divorce in the easiest thing to do these days. One might think of marriage as being similar to buying merchandise and once dissatisfied with its content we return it. It appears harmless on the surface at times but everything is not what it seems. Many get into marriage unadvisedly, thinking "if it does not work out I would just get rid of it and continue my pursuit for the right person". The truth is it is not that easy. Each party does not leave the marriage the same way they entered. Quite often, divorcees enter subsequent marriages with fragments of their ex still a part of them because the union did not just take place physically but emotionally, psychologically and spiritually. Therefore, a powerful soul tie was formed. So can you imagine the faulty foundation being set for the new marriage when the divorcee attempts to enter the marriage bed with a third party (the ex)? It sets up the perfect scenario for chaos and confusion.

As I was evaluating, the words defining marriage, another profound aspect took center stage: marriage is a PROCESS. Marrying one person to another is not instant as is the perception among many but it takes time. The wedding is only the beginning of the marriage. For the two to be soldered, welded together, melted into each other, it takes time. I love the definitive words, *to knit, to chain, lock, pin, nail, bolt, clasp, crimp, screw, solder, set, weld together, fuse together, wedge, absorb, melt into one,* because they drive home the truth that an external and seemingly adverse factor is needed to facilitate the marrying of the two entities. Let me explain; to facilitate knitting a needle is needed (painful, unpleasant yet necessary), to facilitate nailing a hammer is needed, to facilitate screwing together a screwdriver is needed, to facilitate melting together a fire is needed. These are all uncomfortable, painful, unpleasant circumstances yet they are necessary if the separate entities are to married/united with each other seamlessly. This is where most of us quit and run. Many give up *during the marrying process.* I am just as guilty because many times, I would love to have a problem-free marriage. Paul puts it this way:

> *But if you do marry, you have not sinned; and if a virgin marries, she has not sinned.* **But those who marry will face many troubles in this life** . . . . *(Emphasis added)*

1 Cor. 7:28

Now please take note that this is by no means discouraging marriage. Marriage is wonderful; ordained and endorsed by God. What we need to understand is that there is no problem free marriage. The husband and wife may be from different backgrounds with different personalities, and points of view. There will be disagreements and misunderstandings. However, with every hurdle that they overcome, their marriage will grow stronger.

Effects of Divorce

Divorce is the tool that rips the union of the whole: the PERSON of husband and wife. It leaves a gaping wound which both parties are protective of and are very careful not to let anyone get too close to them for fear of the recurrence of the hurt and betrayal. It also leaves a void which they often seek to fill. It has been observed that many persons who have gone through a first divorce often go through a second and even third. You see, although, the physical split might have occurred, the emotional split has not; there is often post divorce hostility between the two parties. They usually take a very long time to acquire psychological equilibrium and quite often some never do. Couples who are going through or have gone through divorce usually have to cope with such emotions as:

- Anxiety
- Anger
- Sadness
- Exhaustion
- Guilt
- Low self-esteem
- Worry
- Disappointment/frustration
- Loneliness
- Rejection

Many times these feelings are not just experienced by the couple faced with the break up but also those who are close to them; especially their children. Growing up as a child in a Caribbean setting, I have often heard adults quote this proverb: "many hands make light work". It basically means there is greater productivity in unity. Two persons working together on a particular task is always better than one person working at it. Divorce, although it appears to have many benefits at the time, demands more from the couple mentally, emotionally, physically and financially. It brings with it added responsibilities and roles particularly with regard to the children. Each parent has to now become both mother and father at any given time. Home is now redefined and very much alternate for the children: they are either in the care of mommy or daddy. There is also a demand for greater financial support since both parties now have to maintain their individual homes and the children. In some instances where the mother was a stay-at-home mom, she is forced to seek employment in order to support herself and children. It has been found that in many divorce situations, the children are the ones who are most affected psychologically. They are usually the unfortunate victims of the quarrels and hostility between their parents. Many of these children have many questions which their parents may prefer not to be asked or are just not ready to discuss. Quite often the children assume that the break up was their fault and many of them take this guilt with them way into their adult years.

Lots of these children develop a negative attitude towards their parents, a particular parent or their marriages if their experience was not dealt with properly. What is very disturbing due to its epidemic proportion, is the number of children who have become victims of physical and sexual abuse from a subsequent relationship into which one of their parents has entered following a divorce or break up (we will look into this in more detail in Part 2).

Some of the effects which divorces have on children are:

- They may feel unwanted and unloved by their parents
- In some cases they are separated from other siblings
- Many blame themselves for their parents' divorce and also live with the hope and expectation that their parents will reunite but when this does not happen, they tend to live with disappointment and anger.
- Lack of concentration on studies resulting in poor academic achievement
- Some children tend to act out their frustrations; negative behaviors and attitude
- Abuse

The bottom line is, divorce does not leave persons whole. Instead, they are left infirmed. It is not God's desire that we live with infirmities in our lives. Jesus Christ took all our infirmities upon himself on the cross that we might live full lives. He told us this in John 10:10:

> *The thief comes only in order to steal and kill and destroy. I came that they may have and enjoy life, and have it in abundance (to the full, till it overflows).*

Reasons for Divorce

It must be understood that despite the numerous causes and grounds for divorce presented today, the basic reason is SIN. Sin in itself is a separating factor in a relationship. It separates us from God and it separates us from each other.

> *for all have sinned and fall short of the glory of God,*
>
> **Rom 3:23**

Sin serves as gap between us and God. It breaks the fellowship between us. Thank God our Father for Jesus Christ His son who has bridged the gap and has reconciled us to Himself. Confession of sins and forgiveness restores the right relationship according to 1 John 1:9

> *If we [freely] admit that we have sinned and confess our sins, He is faithful and just (true to His own nature and promises) and will forgive our sins [dismiss our lawlessness] and [continuously] cleanse us from all unrighteousness [everything not in conformity to His will in purpose, thought, and action].*

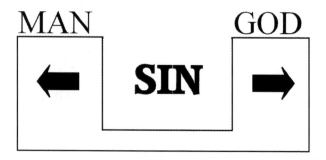

Illustration A: *Sin breaks man's relationship/fellowship with God*

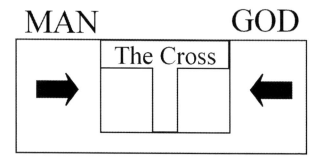

Illustration B: *The removal/forgiveness of sin restores fellowship and right relationship between God and man.*

In the same way, sin affects our relationship with each other and even the relationship between husband and wife.

Jesus said that Moses permitted divorce because of the hardness of the people's heart. The hardness of heart mentioned here is the same as stubbornness. 1Samuel 15:23 says "Rebellion is as sinful as witchcraft and stubbornness as bad as worshiping idols . . . . ." Some may say they fail to see the connection between stubbornness and idolatry since there are no idols involved. Well, actually, there is an idol involved: that idol is ones 'SELF'. As long as we are insisting on our way, our desires, our will, we are actually exalting ourselves above God and we all know how God feels about rivals. He said we must have no other god before Him for He is a jealous God. Stubbornness may be manifested in the form of anger, hatred, bitterness, malice and unforgiveness. It arises when one party feels they have been unjustly treated by the other. Unless the particular issue is quickly dealt with and forgiveness takes place, that marriage would deteriorate.

Some of the popular reasons for divorce in our societies and shamefully in the church are:

- Financial difficulties
- Abuse
- Sexual problems which include adultery, homosexuality, incest
- Immaturity—Some persons are not ready to settle down with just one person for the rest of their lives
- Jealously and control
- Media induced expectation of the "Happily Ever After" factor
- Extra marital influence: it is appalling how many marital problems are credited to the negative influence of in-laws, friends and even trusted religious leaders who have failed to give godly counsel
- Some claim to have grown apart from each other
- the cliché "irreconcilable differences"

In a survey conducted, six out seven persons agreed that the most popular reasons for divorces today are sexual problems, abuse and financial difficulties. This brings us back to the sin problem where the flesh dominates. Paul says in Colossian 3:5 that we are to mortify or put to death. Since we are dead in Christ these things ought not to be found in our lives. The truth is divorce should not be at issue for the child of God but the reality is that as in the days of Moses and Jesus it is prevalent among believers and, therefore, must be addressed. Many people because they become depressed, feel trapped and helpless in their marriages. They have already been mentally and emotionally divorced from the union because consciously or unconsciously they refuse to make any additional investment to the development of the relationship.

Some, in remaining, have contracted STDs from promiscuous spouses and some even died from various forms of domestic abuse because of misinterpretations and insufficient knowledge regarding the biblical position on divorce or what God has created them to be.

Determining Justification: Divorce in the Old Testament

[iv]Under the Mosaic Covenant, a concession was made for a man to divorce his wife.

> *1 WHEN A man takes a wife and marries her, if then*
> *she finds no favor in his eyes because he has found some*
> *indecency in her, and he writes her a bill of divorce,*
> *puts it in her hand, and sends her out of his house,*
>
> *2 And when she departs out of his house*
> *she goes and marries another man,*
>
> *3 And if the latter husband dislikes her and writes her a bill*
> *of divorce and puts it in her hand and sends her out of his*
> *house, or if the latter husband dies, who took her as his wife,*
>
> *4 Then her former husband, who sent her away,*
> *may not take her again to be his wife after she is*
> *defiled. For that is an abomination before the Lord;*
> *and you shall not bring guilt upon the land which*
> *the Lord your God gives you as an inheritance.*

Deut 24:1-4

Moses' concession of the husband giving the wife a bill of divorce was not in any way to encourage divorce or make it easier; rather it was an attempt to regulate and consequently discourage a problem that was widespread. Evidently, his intention was to favor the wife, as far as possible, by protecting her from unlawful expulsion from her home and children. You see, in ancient times as in some modern day cultures, women were viewed and treated as second class citizens and inferior to her male counterpart. Although, Hebrew women were treated considerably better than women of other lands at the time, they were still inferior and subjected in their society. In the Hebrew legislation, the marriage relationship was nothing more than a business transaction, a legal contract and she was the possession/property of her husband. If for any reason he was not pleased with her (his property), he would send her back to her father's house. Moses' law clearly dictates that under certain circumstances, a husband might divorce his wife while on the other hand; it was very difficult, if at all possible for a wife to divorce her husband. This double standard clearly locked the woman in the minority position as it relates to divorce. Moses' concession ensured that by giving the wife a bill of divorce[3], the husband's right to the dowry[4] which the wife brought to the marriage is nullified. In my research, I found that the father of the bride usually gave her a portion which becomes the property of her husband, and which often makes up a considerable part of his wealth. It is supposed that prior to the concession for the bill of divorce being given; the husbands would put away their wives but hold on to the dowry.

Apart from leaving the wife with the dowry, the bill of divorce also afforded her the opportunity to marry another man. With her

---

3   Same as a **Certificate of Divorce** found in Deut. 24:1,3; Is. 50:1; Jer. 3:8 and is translated from the Hebrew cepher kerithuth which signifies a document or book of cutting off.

4   **Dowry"** generally refers to the gift that a bride brought to marriage. The groom also brought a gift, the moehar (AV "dowry"; RSV "marriage present"; NEB "bride-price"), which was paid to the bride's father as compensation for the loss of a daughter. This "marriage present" was very important, for it sealed the betrothal (cf. Ex 22:17). (from International Standard Bible Encyclopedia, revised edition, Copyright © 1979 by Wm. B. Eerdmans Publishing Co. All rights reserved.)

subjugated role in society, the wife could not divorce her husband but she could force him to divorce her by being intolerably burdensome to him; in other words, make his life miserable.

Although, the divorce procedure according to Moses' law seemed more in favor of the husband, it made it as difficult as possible for him to secure a divorce. No husband could have obtained a divorce from his wife without some semblance of a trial. As I mentioned earlier, prior to the implementing of this law, the men of Israel were getting rid of their wives for all kinds of unjustifiable reasons, taking their directives from specifications outlined in certain rabbinic literal. Some of these specifications regarding a woman who could be divorced, taken from the Mishnah[5] included:

- The spoiling of a dish either by burning or careless seasoning.
- If he found another woman whom he liked better, or who was more beautiful
- If she violates the Law of Moses.
- If she vowed and did not keep it or if she went into the street with her hair loose, or spins in the street
- If she is a noisy woman i.e. one who speaks in her own house so loudly that the neighbor could hear her.

As a result of the Mosaic Law, a husband who became dissatisfied with his wife was required to:

1. Write her a Certificate of Divorce
2. This certificate of divorce had to be placed in the hand of the divorced wife
3. She must be forced to leave the premises of her former husband

---

[5] **Mishna**—the first part of the Talmud; a collection of early oral interpretations of the scriptures that was compiled about AD200 (information taken from: http://www.biblestudytools.com/dictionaries/bakers-evangelical-dictionary/divorce.html)

In addition, divorce was denied to two types of men:

1. The man who accuses his wife falsely of infidelity (Deut. 22:13) and
2. The man who seduced a virgin (Deut 22:28) he had to pay a heavy fine to the father of the young woman.

All of these regulations and stipulations existed in the Mosaic legislation of divorce and as was in the case of the entire law; served as our tutor to bring us to Christ (Gal 3:24).

Determining Justification: Divorce in the New Testament

> *3 The Pharisees also came to Him, testing Him, and saying to Him, "Is it lawful for a man to divorce his wife for just any reason?"*
>
> *4 And He answered and said to them, "Have you not read that He who made them at the beginning 'made them male and female,'*
>
> *5 and said, 'For this reason a man shall leave his father and mother and be joined to his wife, and the two shall become one flesh'?*
>
> *6 So then, they are no longer two but one flesh. Therefore what God has joined together, let not man separate."*
>
> *7 They said to Him, "Why then did Moses command to give a certificate of divorce, and to put her away?"*
>
> *8 He said to them, "Moses, **because of the hardness of your hearts, permitted you to divorce your wives,** but from the beginning it was not so. 9 And I say to you, whoever divorces his wife, except for sexual immorality,*

*and marries another, commits adultery; and whoever
marries her who is divorced commits adultery."*

Matt 19:3-9

We cannot determine the allowance and divine validity of
divorce without taking into consideration what Jesus Christ
taught concerning it since He is the fulfillment of the law and
gave true interpretation to the moral precepts of the commands
given to us. He brought clarity to the subject of divorce and it
is His word that we must follow. We must always bear in mind
that Jesus Christ is the Word (John 1:1), the Logos, the FULL
counsel of God.

Moses made a concession for divorce in an attempt to regulate
and hopefully mitigate it whereas Jesus with the full authority of
His father issued commands concerning it. The people of the day
as some do today held the words/laws of Moses in high esteem. We
see in biblical account how often times they were willing to kill their
very own to preserve it even though it had become null and void as
a result of Christ. On the Mount of Transfiguration, as it is called,
God the Father made a declaration which established a distinct
demarcation of the authority of Jesus Christ and the words He spoke
when compared with other speakers/writers.

*17 After six days Jesus took with him Peter, James and
John the brother of James, and led them up a high
mountain by themselves. 2 There he was transfigured
before them. His face shone like the sun, and his clothes
became as white as the light. 3 Just then there appeared
before them Moses and Elijah, talking with Jesus.*

*4 Peter said to Jesus, "Lord, it is good for us to be
here. If you wish, I will put up three shelters—one
for you, one for Moses and one for Elijah."*

5 While he was still speaking, a bright cloud enveloped them, and a voice from the cloud said, "This is my Son, whom I love; with him I am well pleased. Listen to him!"

6 When the disciples heard this, they fell facedown to the ground, terrified. 7 But Jesus came and touched them. "Get up," he said. "Don't be afraid." 8 When they looked up, they saw no one except Jesus.

Matt 17:1-8

One day while Peter, James and John were on the mountain with Jesus, Moses and Elijah appeared and spoke with him. Peter was excited and amazed by this remarkable experience and suggested that three tabernacles (monuments) be erected in honor of all three. Now Elijah and Moses were both powerfully anointed and legitimate servants of God but they were not the Christ[6]. Immediately, God the Father intervened and affirmed the divine identity of Jesus and the authority of the words He speaks; "this is my beloved Son . . . . listen to Him" (Matt. 17:5). When the disciples looked up the only person they saw was Jesus; Elijah was gone, Moses was gone. What is this saying? It means Jesus is exalted far above all else. How often do we not downplay the 'truth' (the word of God) and esteem the philosophies of seemingly intellectual 'mortal' men of God? The words that God speaks through His servants will always exalt Christ and will be the words Jesus speaks. His words which include the commands about divorce are above all other words. So the Old Testament divorce structure has become a mere letter and not applicable to our dispensation.

In the conversation between Jesus and the Pharisees, He brought clarity to the whole divorce issue. Ever since the times of Moses, many

---

[6]   **Christos**—this is the Hebrew word for Christ and it means "anointed". He was the Messiah, the Son of God. In him was the anointing without measure.

of the leaders agree that there were some circumstances that require separation in marriage but determining justifiable grounds was always the argument. Jesus established that according to the purpose of God, marriage was a covenant not to be broken. As we have seen, He pointed out Moses' reason for giving the concession of divorce which was as a result of the hardness of their hearts (stubbornness to their own way). God is a covenant keeping God and He expected from the beginning and still expects that His people honor their marriage covenant to each other but He allowed Moses to give a concession to the people. I firmly believe that we will always reap the maximum benefits of marriage if we choose to walk in God's original intent. His perfect will, for the covenant of marriage made no accommodation for divorce. However, with consideration of sin and human frailty, there is the choice of a concession given. It is always in our best interest to choose to walk in the perfect will of God. However, it takes a renewed mind to prove the acceptable and perfect will of God (Romans 12:2). This is the problem; many times we do not want to accept the word of God and allow it to change us. We try to merge the word of God with our philosophies and opinions. Trying to merge the old and new makes the new ineffective in our lives much like the new wine being poured into old wineskin; thus, bursting the skin and spilling the new wine. Change is hard but it is necessary. Therefore let us seek to renew our minds daily by heeding to the word of God.

Within the context of Jesus' response to the questions posted to Him, He address issues of divorce, remarriage and also redefined adultery. Adultery according to Jewish law had a different meaning from what we know it to be today. In the Jewish context of marriage, polygamy[7] and concubinage[8] were legitimate. A Hebrew man who

---

[7]   **Polygamy** is the condition or practice of having more than one spouse at one time

[8]   **Concubinage** is the state of being or keeping a concubine who is a woman who is the lover of a wealthy married man but with the social status of a subordinate form of wife, often kept in a separate home

was married, could have had two or more wives, also concubines and might have intercourse with a slave or bondwoman, without being guilty of adultery (Leviticus 19:20). According to Jewish law, the only time a married man is possibly guilty of adultery is when he dishonored the free wife of a Hebrew (Leviticus 20:10). Now Jesus came on the scene and said "this is what you have heard and are used to but this is what I am saying to you now . . . ." (Paraphrased), therefore, this is what you are expected to follow. In Matthew 5:27, 28, He says "You have heard that it was said, 'Do not commit adultery.' *But I tell you* that anyone who looks at a woman lustfully has already committed adultery with her in his heart" NIV. Here in Matthew 19:9, He is bringing greater clarity to the definition of adultery by stating that the person who divorces and marries another person for any other reason apart from sexual immorality is committing adultery. There are so many explanations and opinions on this subject of whether or not God permits a Christian to divorce. I am no expert on this subject but with the leading of the Holy Spirit, I will attempt to address it. When God instituted marriage, divorce was never a part of the package. However, because of sin and the hardness of man's heart, Moses made a concession for a bill of divorce to be given. Here in Matthew 19, Jesus did not annul the permission for divorce. Instead He brought clarity and definition to it. The ground for the divorce determines the validity of remarriage in that, unless the divorce is because of sexual immorality (fornication), marrying a new person is an adulterous affair.

At this point another issue comes to mind; and that's regarding the divorce that is spoken of not being from the actually consummated marriage but rather it was from the betrothal. In Hebrew culture, before two people were actually married, they were betrothed (meaning to promise "by one's truth") to each other which was quite different from our context of engagement. According to Nelson's Bible Dictionary, the bride was first selected then the betrothal took place. It was undertaken by a friend or agent representing the bridegroom and by the parents representing the bride. It was confirmed by oaths and was accompanied with presents to the bride and often to the bride's parents then celebrated by a feast. In some instances, the bridegroom would place a ring or a token of his love and fidelity on the bride's finger. The betrothal was a part of the marriage process and usually lasted about twelve months. Although it was not the actual marriage, in the Hebrew culture the two people were legally considered husband and wife although sexual union was prohibited until the actual marriage. The actual marriage took place when the husband took his wife to his home and consummated the marriage. The only way a Jewish betrothal could have been dissolved, was by the husband giving the wife a bill of divorce. Hence, we can see the argument regarding the concession of divorce being spoken about in Matthew 19 and the Hebrew context at large. If we look closely, we would see that the marriage spoken of, whether the betrothal or consummated marriage was not specified, so it would be inconclusive to say that the concession of divorce was just from the betrothal. Earlier, I mentioned that according to Jewish law, there were two types of men who could not receive a divorce; one of which was the one who seduced a virgin who was not betrothed.

28 If a man finds a girl who is a virgin, who is not betrothed, and he seizes her and lies with her and they are found,

29 Then the man who lay with her shall give to the girl's father fifty shekels of silver, and she shall be his wife, because he has violated her; **he may not divorce her all his days.**

Deut 22:28-29

It is significant that the author emphasized that this particular man could not obtain a divorce all the days of his life which means that some men were allowed to divorce at different points in the marriage which was not restricted to the betrothal which was usually for a twelve months period. Also, in Jesus' initial response to the Pharisees recapping God's original intent, He pointed out that *the two become one*, the man *leaves* father and mother and *cleaves* to his wife. I believe this is referring to the actual consummated marriage when the husband is joined to his wife.

True, there are other accounts of what Jesus said, in Mark 10:2-12 and Luke 16:18, but Matthew 19 gives the fullest account of all He said. Some persons argue that the other writers did not mention ". . . . and I say unto you, whosoever shall put away his wife, **except it be for fornication** . . . . ." therefore, it is most likely not applicable. It is not known for certain why two writers failed to include it while another writer did; however, Matthew is believed to be more thorough in his report of Jesus' teachings and sayings. Also, there is another factor which we should consider: Mark and Luke were not personal disciples of Jesus so their reports were more of a second hand report and are likely to be more of a summary of that which was told to them. This increases the possibility of some details being excluded. On the other hand, Matthew was a personal disciple of Jesus writing a firsthand report of what he had witnessed, seen and heard.

If we should all accept and follow carefully what Jesus taught, we would all think carefully before pursuing a divorce and even more carefully before entering into marriage unadvisedly.

Chapter Highlights

- Divorce is a perversion of the marriage institution which God ordained for His glory.
- To marry means to tie, to string, to strap, to stitch, to knit, to chain, lock, pin, nail, bolt, clasp, crimp, screw, solder, set, weld together, fuse together, wedge, absorb, melt into one, and to cement a union.
- Separating the seamless union of marriage cannot occur without one or both parties being damaged in the process.
- Marriage is a process
- An external and seemingly adverse factor is needed to facilitate the marrying of the two entities.
- Change is hard but it is necessary.

CHAPTER FOUR

DEALING WITH THE AFTERMATH

*But He said to me, My grace (My favor and loving-kindness and mercy) is enough for you [sufficient against any danger and enables you to bear the trouble manfully]; for My strength and power are made perfect (fulfilled and completed) and show themselves most effective in [your] weakness . . . . **2 Cor 12:9***

A divorce can be very traumatic; leaving a wake of devastation in its path. It can be one of the most frightening and challenging experience for a person as he or she attempts to pick up the pieces of their broken lives. If you are going through a divorce or have gone through one, you have my prayer because you are likely to experience feelings of fear, distrust, grief, anger, betrayal, bewilderment and other similar emotions. For me to say that I know what you are going through would be to trivialize your experience which would be very insensitive and unreasonable. Although there may be some similarities, every situation is different from the other as is each person's response to them. I have never experienced divorce, although, I came very close to it. My husband and I have separated more times than I can remember and I can truly say that it is only by the grace of God that we are still together and for this we ascribe all glory to His matchless name. The heartbreak and pains that come as a result of these crises are beyond words and you always wish that you never had to deal with them. It becomes even harder when a child or children are involved. I understand the difficulty of trying to juggle dealing with the hurts of your children and your own while being faced with their questions which forces you to face a reality you would rather forget. In as much as there is no one who can truly identify with what you are going through and how you feel as an individual, I would like you to know that there is someone who knows exactly how you feel; His name is Jesus Christ. This is what the Bible says:

> *15 For we do not have a High Priest Who is unable to understand and sympathize and have a shared feeling with our weaknesses and infirmities and liability to the assaults of temptation, but One Who has been tempted in every respect as we are, yet without sinning.*
>
> *16 Let us then fearlessly and confidently and boldly draw near to the throne of grace (the throne of God's unmerited favor to us sinners), that we may receive mercy [for our failures] and find grace to help in good time for every need [appropriate help and well-timed help, coming just when we need it].*

Heb 4:15-16

Jesus is familiar with every trial and hardship we go through. The church has a tendency to treat persons who have been divorced with contempt. I am very thankful that we serve a merciful and loving God who sits on His throne forever and can never be over thrown because if many of us could be God we would exempt a lot of persons from eternal life. The bottom line is that no matter what you have done or are facing you can approach the throne of grace boldly, pour out your heart to Him and He will shower you with mercy. There is nothing too hard for the Lord.

In speaking with persons over the years, I have come to realize that amidst all the concerns about divorce, there are some pertinent ones. I will attempt to address some of these questions based on personal encounters, experiences and most importantly, with the help of the Holy Spirit.

How do I cope with hardships resulting from divorce such as physical needs, financial struggles, emotional hurts and the effects on my spiritual life?

The consequences of divorce are many and truly affect every aspect of a person's life. I strongly recommend not only on my authority but on the authority of the word of God, that you focus firstly on the spiritual aspect before attempting to deal with the others. At this point in your life, you definitely need to prioritize because it is easy to become overwhelmed by the flood of emotions and demands.

25 "Therefore I say to you, do not worry about your life, what you will eat or what you will drink; nor about your body, what you will put on. Is not life more than food and the body more than clothing? 26 Look at the birds of the air, for they neither sow nor reap nor gather into barns; yet your heavenly Father feeds them. Are you not of more value than they? 27 Which of you by worrying can add one cubit to his stature?

28 "So why do you worry about clothing? Consider the lilies of the field, how they grow: they neither toil nor spin; 29 and yet I say to you that even Solomon in all his glory was not arrayed like one of these. 30 Now if God so clothes the grass of the field, which today is, and tomorrow is thrown into the oven, will He not much more clothe you, O you of little faith?

31 "Therefore do not worry, saying, 'What shall we eat?' or 'What shall we drink?' or 'What shall we wear?' 32 For after all these things the Gentiles seek. For your heavenly Father knows that you need all these things. 33 But seek first the kingdom of God and His righteousness, and all these things shall be added to you. 34 Therefore do not worry about tomorrow, for tomorrow will worry about its own things. Sufficient for the day is its own trouble.

Matt 6:25-34

In Matthew chapter six, Jesus admonishes us to prioritize. If our priorities are in order it would eliminate the need to worry. At the top of our list of priorities must be the kingdom of God (His rule) and His righteousness (having right relationship with Him), then everything else will be added to you. You need to remember God is the source and all things come from Him. If you seek Him you will receive Him and everything that comes with Him including health, wealth, sound mind and hope. He rewards those who diligently seek Him. The reward of any search is to find the thing or the person you are looking for. In this case the reward of the search is God Himself and everything that comes with Him.

I recently went through a divorce and have lost all desire to socialize or get involved in any activity. I just feel like being alone all the time and have even stopped going to church. Is this normal behavior for someone in my situation?

It is not unusual for a person who has experience deep hurts and betrayal such as those associated with divorce to feel the need to isolate him or herself from the rest of the world. However, I would not encourage you to resort to that. In my view, using total isolation as an escape route from your reality provides the perfect nesting ground for depression and even suicidal thoughts. It is in those times that the battle in your mind intensifies. You definitely need to be connected with positive people: other believers who would be able to encourage and strengthen you. It is in this family setting, in this atmosphere of unity that healing and wholeness flows.

1 BEHOLD, HOW good and how pleasant it
is for brethren to dwell together in unity!

2 It is like the precious ointment poured on the head,
that ran down on the beard, even the beard of Aaron [the

*first high priest], that came down upon the collar and
skirts of his garments [consecrating the whole body].*

*3 It is like the dew of [lofty] Mount Hermon and
the dew that comes on the hills of Zion; for there
the Lord has commanded the blessing, even life
forevermore [upon the high and the lowly].*

Ps 133

Where brethrens assemble in unity having common focus, common passion, common desire, God commands His blessing and life. In such an assemblage, depression, frustration and self pity have to leave, for such an atmosphere is saturated with love, freedom and encouragement. When you connect with the right people, you will recover faster than if you remain in isolation.

How am I supposed to relate to my ex after all that has happened? I do not have a problem if he wants to speak to the children but I would rather not have anything to do with him whatsoever.

Communicating with or even being in the same room with an ex-spouse could be very challenging since there may be anger, resentment, unforgiveness and other unresolved feelings still present. However, the two of you must be able to communicate, especially if there are children involved. Both of you must bear in mind that you are not the only ones being affected by the divorce but your children are the innocent parties in this and you must be sensitive to their needs. You must be able to communicate at least concerning; visitation and financial support.

Also, I know this would be hard for you to accept right now but if you are going to be truly free to move on, free from the shackles of torment, you need to forgive him. As long as you are still angered by the presence of your ex, by the sound of his voice, even at the mention of his name, you have not forgiven. Forgiveness will release you to walk in newness and help to bring healing to you. Therefore, forgiveness at this point in time is more beneficial for you than for him. *(For more on forgiveness read chapter 12)*

What should the response of the church be towards divorcees or those on the brink of a divorce?

Romans 3:23 says that all of us have sinned and fallen short of God's glorious standards. Without exemption, we have all failed God some time or other. It tells me that if our salvation was dependent on us meeting the standards of God, all of us would be going to hell, from the pulpit to the pew. Since we have been saved by grace and not by any good works we have no right to look down on our fellow brothers and sisters as if they are less righteous. If anyone considers him or herself more spiritual, they have the responsibility of restoring, helping, nurturing, those who have fallen and to do so in love because you may need someone to love and restore you sooner than you think.

> *Brethren, if a man is overtaken in any trespass,*
> *you who are spiritual restore such a one in a spirit*
> *of gentleness, considering yourself lest you also be*
> *tempted. 2 Bear one another's burdens, and so fulfill*
> *the law of Christ. 3 For if anyone thinks himself to be*
> *something, when he is nothing, he deceives himself.*

Gal 6:1-4

If we are children of God, we must exhibit the attribute of our Father. Love motivated Him to send His only son to die so we can be restored to right relationship with Him; to restore us to 'sonship'. Everything we do in the Body of Christ must be fueled by love.

Should a divorcee be permitted to function in the church?

I do believe that an individual should not be prohibited from functioning within the church on the basis of them being divorced. I know of many anointed men and women of God who have gone through a divorce yet God continues to use them mightily for the glory and honor of His name. If God does not condemn them then why should the rest of us. He has given them gifts which He expects them to use.

As each one has received a gift, minister it to one another,
as good stewards of the manifold grace of God.

1 Peter 4:10

Furthermore, God is not impressed nor moved by how gifted we think we are or how long we have been saved or how much we think we have done for the church. He is looking for availability; persons who would be obedient to Him, person's who will be willing to put His will above their own desires and ambitions. He seeks a person in whom and through whom He can establish His kingdom and if that's a divorcee so be it.

The fact that you have not died nor lost your mind, tells me that God is with you and has kept you for a reason; your life is not over. I am saying this not just for those faced with divorce but I am also speaking to those of you who have been encountering or have come through some really trying situations. God favored you! This is your time for renewal. It's not over!

Chapter Highlights

- Prioritizing eliminates the need to worry
- At the top of our list of priorities must be the Kingdom of God (His rule) and His righteousness (having right relationship with Him), then everything else will be added to you.
- God rewards those who diligently seek Him
- The reward of the search is God Himself and everything that comes with Him.
- In an atmosphere of unity, healing and wholeness flows
- Connecting with the right people encourages faster recovery from the hurts and pains of divorce
- Everything we do in the Body of Christ must be fueled by love.
- He seeks a person in whom and through whom he can establish His kingdom

CHAPTER FIVE

REMARRIAGE

And I say unto you, Whosoever shall put away his wife, except it be for fornication, and shall marry another, committeth adultery: and whoso marrieth her which is put away doth commit adultery. **Matt 19:9**

Is remarriage permitted by God? This question has plagued the mind of many in the Christian community. We have been exposed to ministries that bluntly refuse to remarry divorcees while others have taken the liberty to reinterpret and act upon their belief by remarrying divorcees and even permitting ministers of the gospel to have second marriages themselves. Clearly, divorce among others such as: the correct day to worship, clean and unclean foods and the manifestations of the Holy Spirit, have all been contributing factors to segregation in the Body of Christ; thus disrupting the harmony of the church (Romans 14:19).

Jesus said unless the divorce was as a result of fornication, any marriage which follows will be an act of adultery and, therefore, unlawful. As was stated earlier, he did not prohibit divorce or annulled the concession made by Moses' for divorce. His response to the Pharisees' question gives a clear indication that if a person is divorced for any other reason apart from that which falls under "*fornication*" that person should be prepared to remain single, reconcile with their spouse or commit an act of adultery by marrying someone else. I know what would arise in some minds at this point is the question of what is fornication? When we hear of fornication the first definition that usually comes to mind is sex outside of marriage and this answer is correct. However, there is much more to what fornication is all about. Using our understanding of fornication, we can see that adultery is an act of fornication (since the individuals are not married to each other) while on the other hand, not all acts of fornication are adultery; simply because not all fornicators are married to someone. Fornication includes various aspects of sexual immorality. The word used in this context in Matthew 19:9 is the Greek word ᵛ"Porneia" which when translated into English means illicit sexual intercourse:

a. adultery, fornication, homosexuality, lesbianism, intercourse with animals etc.
b. sexual intercourse with close relatives; Lev. 18
c. sexual intercourse with a divorced man or woman; Mk. 10:11,

Porneia is also used metaphorically in the Bible in reference to the worship of idols. In the Book of Revelation, fornication is symbolic of how idolatry and pagan religion defiles the true worship of God (Rev 14:8; 17:4) (Nelson, 1986). According to Fausset's Bible Dictionary, it also refers to spiritual unfaithfulness to the Lord, Israel's and the church's husband (Ezek 16; Jer. 2:1; Hos 1:1; Rev 17:4).

The Apostle Paul also spoke on the subject of marriage and the believer's responsibility in and towards marriage. Apart from Jesus, Paul was the only other New Testament author who spoke about marriage, divorce and remarriage and he did so not in himself but under the apostolic authority; accompanying wisdom given to him by God. Although he addresses certain areas of marriage which Jesus never spoke about, it is important to note that he did not modify that which was already spoken by Christ in any way. As a matter of fact, in 1 Corinthians 7:10-11, Paul affirmed Jesus' statement concerning God's original intent for marriage when he said it is a command from God that the two must not divorce.

10 But to the married people I give charge—not I but the
Lord—that the wife is not to separate from her husband.

11 But if she does [separate from and divorce him],
let her remain single or else be reconciled to her
husband. And [I charge] the husband [also] that
he should not put away or divorce his wife.

1 Cor 7:10-11

Paul considered the sin factor and acknowledged as Moses did the possibility of divorce and further stated that if they do divorce, let them remain as they are and not remarry. Looking closely at Paul's letter to the Corinthians, we find that he never really discussed the issue of the grounds for divorce. In 1 Corinthians 7:15, he made a concession regarding the marriage between a believer and an unbeliever.

But if the unbelieving partner [actually] leaves, let him
do so; in such [cases the remaining] brother or sister is
not morally bound. But God has called us to peace.

1 Cor 7:15

He said if the unbelieving spouse insists on leaving the marriage, the believing one should let them go. Although, we can clearly suppose that this desertion can be considered grounds for divorce, he in no way said that the believer may remarry. In fact, Paul's main theme throughout 1 Corinthians chapter 7 is urging the believers to remain in or accept the situation in which God has called them: if you were married (for example to an unbeliever) do not seek to leave because you are now saved, if single do not seek to be married unless you have no self control, if divorced do not seek to remarry.

Jesus says "**Whosoever shall put away his wife**, except it be for fornication . . . ." i.e. the one who breaks the covenant of marriage for any other reason apart from fornication shows by his action that he does not understand and does not accept God's original intent for marriage. It would be unwise for a person with such a disposition to remarry since he/she is likely to repeat the act. Until there is a renewing of the mind, the person will remain the same thus behaving in the same manner. The relationship of the Godhead must be reflected in marriages. God who honors covenant expects that we do the same as His children. Even in marriages, God's will, intent, desires and purposes must be exalted above our own.

Divorce is indicative of the hardness of man's heart and intent to have his will prevail against God's in the marriage. Stubbornness causes a person to reject the word of God. If you are divorced, as Paul says, it is better to remain single where you can focus on the things that concern God.

After careful examination of all that Jesus said to the Pharisees, the disciples felt and expressed as Paul later did, that it is, better not to marry. Many church goers/believers struggle with the issue of divorce and remarriage and have sought the advice and opinions of learned figures to the point where we even questioned God regarding the numerous debates on the subject. Are we just wrestling with the truth that is right before us because it is not what we want to hear? As I continued reading verse 11 of Matthew 19, what Jesus said next in response to the disciples really hit home; he said "not everyone can accept this word". What word was he talking about? The word he is speaking about is concerning marriage. You see, to be married to someone is not an easy act. It takes maturity, the fear of the Lord and grace (divine enablement). We cannot do it by ourselves; just look around at the many evidences of it in the church. God gives grace to the humble, those who submit to His rule, those who are willing to say "not my will but yours be done." He releases His angels to minister strength to us when we take such a stand. Marriage is not for everyone. Those who can take it should accept it. We must understand that our marriages cannot make it without God; He is the source from which it came. Therefore, if our marriages are detached from the source (foundation, inspiration, life, and sustenance) they will die!

Chapter Highlights

- The relationship of the Godhead must be reflected in marriages
- God's will, intent, desires and purposes must be exalted above ours in marriages.
- Stubbornness causes a person to reject the word of God.
- Divorce is indicative of the hardness of man's heart and intent to have his will prevail against God's in the marriage.
- We must understand that our marriages cannot make it without God; He is the source from which it came.
- If our marriages are detached from the source (foundation, inspiration, life, sustenance) they will die.

CHAPTER SIX

THE ROAD TO SUCCESS

*"Forgiveness is the most powerful thing you can do for yourself.
If you can't learn to forgive, you can forget about achieving true
success in your life."*—**Dr. Dyer**

*27 So God created man in His own image; in the image
of God He created him; male and female He created them.
28 Then God blessed them, and God said to them, "Be
fruitful and multiply; fill the earth and subdue it; have
dominion over the fish of the sea, over the birds of the air,
and over every living thing that moves on the earth."*

Gen 1:27-28

There is a corporate anointing (grace, divine empowerment) given
to marriage by God to carry out a corporate mandate. This mandate
is one of dominion thus filling the earth with a God-infused,
God-inspired race. The two becoming one is meant to operate in
the principle of being in one accord having one mind, one heart;
though each is unique and productive in his or her own right;
yet they find greater purpose and functionality in the WHOLE.
For those who are married or intend to get married, you must
understand and embrace this principle. Marriage is much more that
companionship and definitely more than sexual pleasure. It is very
important that the bigger picture of God's purpose for marriage be
seen and allowed to define our marriage relationship or else when
the heat rises we will easily succumb to our desire and eventually
join the divorce check-out line. The two persons and by this I am
referring to husband and wife, male and female (just to be clear), in

a marriage must understand who they are and why they exist and were placed together by God. Once this is understood, they become a force that cannot be easily overcome. Such a union, according to Genesis 1:28, is blessed by God and is correctly positioned for increase, expansion, victory and dominion. They understand that their union is a reflection of the image and likeness of the Godhead. They understand that they are God's royal priesthood in the earth therefore, as His representation they cannot be caught up in themselves when they have been charged with a mandate to the earth. They understand that as God's representatives, they stand in the gap, fully representing creation including each other before God and they recognize the devil's devises to divide and conquer them. They see each other through the eyes of God. Such a marriage cannot fail because it is equipped with all that's necessary for success.

Finding the Way Back

The countless manifestation of marital dysfunctions, separations, and divorces are true revelation as to why many are losing hope and confidence in marriage. A few years ago, when you spoke to a young person, often times one of their desires was to get married and have a family. In recent times however, there are many who have lost all desire to get married and some would tell you it's because of the number of failed marriages they have seen, especially in the church. Many of them are actually afraid of making the wrong decision. They look at marriages which they had once viewed as examples fail and think "if it can happen to them, it can happen to anyone". Some Christian young people want to serve God; they want children but do not want to get married for fear of becoming a divorce statistic or being hurt. Eventually, they make a choice which leads them out of the church angry and wounded. Many of them, consequently, suffer much abuse and rejection even from those close to them.

Amidst all of this, there is hope. I do believe there is a way to possibly decrease the divorce rate. I am speaking of counseling. There is an old saying: "prevention is better than cure". That is, instead of having to treat it, it would be better and wiser to implement measure to prevent it from the very beginning.

In an attempt to prevent the high probability of divorce, greater emphasis needs to be placed on premarital counseling. Premarital counseling as we know it needs to change; the couple week's summary/routine talk with the couple will not cut it. The right guidance in making such a decision is very important. For persons who may be contemplating divorce or may be encountering marital problems which seem too much for them to deal with, counseling could prove to be an invaluable tool. If they are Christians, they should speak with their spiritual leader which may be their pastor, so that he is made aware of the situation and give them godly counsel; if he is not equipped to counsel them, he can refer them to a counselor best suited to deal with it.

It is easy for us to tell the woman who has been hurt repeatedly by her husband's unfaithfulness to forgive, but unless she sees and understands the need for forgiveness, she would keep returning to her former state of bitterness and resentment. This is where counseling could be most useful. It aids in bringing that person, in this case the woman, to the place where her mind can be renewed and her quality of living changed to the extent where she can now confront and deal with her situations for herself.

If marriage is going to be rerouted to the path of fulfilling its true purpose which is according to God's original intent, we need to acknowledge the need to seek after and walk in godly counsel. Then, we will be "like a tree planted by the rivers of water bringing forth fruits in season and whatsoever we do will prosper". Godly counsel on marriage channels the marriage to God's purpose for the man and woman and unto the path of success.

Chapter Highlights

- Even though two people become one through marital union and should share one mind and one heart, each is unique in his/her own right. However, they find greater purpose and functionality when they merge their individual productivity to make one WHOLE union.
- For persons who may be contemplating divorce or may be encountering marital crisis counseling could prove to be an invaluable tool.
- If marriage is going to be rerouted to the path of fulfilling its true purpose which is according to God's original intent, we need to acknowledge the need to seek after and walk in godly counsel

PART 2
ABUSE

Chapter Seven

Defining Abuse

Have you ever had something given to you that you end up using for some other reason apart from its true purpose because you were not sure of its purpose? Imagine having something as valuable as a crock pot, for example, and because you are not sure what it is to be used for, you have been using it as storage for knickknacks. Since its purpose is not known nor understood that crock pot is being abused.

Abuse can be defined simply as the abnormal use of something or someone. It is the improper usage or treatment of something apart from its intended purpose. As discussed in section one, God created each of us with a purpose in mind and it's in operating within the parameters of that purpose that we produce maximum results. He has placed within us every gift, talent and creative idea needed to bring that purpose to fruition in our lives. In Jeremiah 29: 11, God says:

> *For I know the plans I have for you," declares*
> *the Lord, "plans to prosper you and not to harm*
> *you, plans to give you hope and a future.*

Jer. 29:11

Operating outside of or being treated contrary to God's purpose for us makes us abusers or victims of abuse. We were not created to be abused. It is a strategy of the devil in using the abuser to devalue the one being abused and to break their spirit. It is an attempt to strip us of our peace of mind, self worth, confidence, strength, joy, hope and future. Abuse is cruel and inhumane. It occurs when one person attempts to control another by capitalizing on their need for intimacy, dependency, and trust.

There are so many persons in society, more so in the church that are living in abusive situations everyday and the sad thing is some of them do not even know it. You may ask, is that even possible? Believe it or not, it is. Some persons are ignorant of what constitutes abuse and therefore accept it as a normal part of their life. They may mistake it for love, concern for their well being and some may even believe that it is what God expects of them. This is why it is so important for us to be knowledgeable of the truth of the God's Word, and His purpose for our lives. There are too many persons in the church who spend little or no time studying the Bible. The most time is spent on Sunday mornings during the worship service. It is imperative for us to know, believe and act upon God's word if we are to overcome the sordid realities of life. The scripture confirms this in Proverbs 25:2 NIV:

It is the glory of God to conceal a matter;
to search out a matter is the glory of kings.

Kings are well informed! To be a king is more than wealth acquisition and the exerting authority. In fact, his authority stems from and is connected to the knowledge he possesses. We get excited about being a 'royal priesthood' and being 'kings and priest with Christ' to the extent where we attach this position to the accumulation of material things when it entails more. You see, kings are not satisfied with living in ignorance or darkness. They passionately pursue truth until they find it.

It is in receiving a revelation of Christ that we would better understand who we are, what we are worth and the authority we possess. If you do not know who you are, the purpose for which you exist and where you are going; you are susceptible to abuse. This is when circumstances and persons who come in your life define you. Darkness or ignorance arms the abuser while light exposes his strategies and strips him of his hold on the victim. It is my prayer that the information made available in this book will equip you with the knowledge you need to make good judgment and break free from abuse.

Chapter Highlights

- Abuse can be defined simply as the <u>ab</u>normal <u>use</u> of something or someone.
- God created each of us with a purpose in mind and it's in operating within the parameters of that purpose that we produce maximum results.
- To be a king is more than wealth acquisition and the exerting authority, as a matter of fact kingly authority stems from and is connected to the knowledge he possessed by the king.
- It is in receiving a revelation of Christ that we would understand who we are, what we are worth; the authority we possess.
- Darkness or ignorance arms the abuser while light exposes his strategies and strips him of his hold on the victim.

Chapter Eight

Reasons for Abuse

The main reasons behind abuse are control, the need to feel powerful and the experience of manipulating others. There are, however, no justifiable reasons for abuse. Each of us was created by God and given the freedom, right and privilege of making choices. Abuse to a great extent involves the control of a person's thoughts, feelings and behavior. It is manipulative, self seeking and is likened unto witchcraft. Many of us hate witchcraft. We know it is evil and we pray against it in our prayer meetings. However, we need to realize that witchcraft is more than hexes and potions. The aim of witchcraft is to control another person; to get them to do and behave how we want them to behave for our benefit. This should really cause us to take a closer look at relationships: domestically, spiritually and on a professional basis. Paul points out in Galatians 5:21 ". . . . those who live like this will not inherit the Kingdom of God". When we set out to manipulate a person, we are setting ourselves up as that person's sovereign authority which is in direct opposition/rebellion to the authority of God.

Looking at abuse manifesting itself, we realize that it occurs on many different levels at home in the workplace and in the church. Manipulation is defined as influence of control, shrewdly or deviously. As leaders, particularly in the Body of Christ we have to be so careful of our methods used in leading God's people and the motives behind them. Abuse when employed in our leadership leaves a set of timid, fearful, unhappy, depressed, and dependant people with stifled potentials and crippled purposes.

There is a foundational reason why abuse occur which I came across in the word of God:

4 So all the elders of Israel gathered together and came to Samuel at Ramah. 5 They said to him, "You are old, and your sons do not walk in your ways; now appoint a king to lead us, such as all the other nations have."

6 But when they said, "Give us a king to lead us," this displeased Samuel; so he prayed to the Lord. 7 And the Lord told him: "Listen to all that the people are saying to you; it is not you they have rejected, but they have rejected me as their king. 8 As they have done from the day I brought them up out of Egypt until this day, forsaking me and serving other gods, so they are doing to you. 9 Now listen to them; but warn them solemnly and let them know what the king who will reign over them will do."

10 Samuel told all the words of the Lord to the people who were asking him for a king. 11 He said, "This is what the king who will reign over you will do: He will take your sons and make them serve with his chariots and horses, and they will run in front of his chariots. 12 Some he will assign to be commanders of thousands and commanders of fifties, and others to plow his ground and reap his harvest, and still others to make weapons of war and equipment for his chariots. 13 He will take your daughters to be perfumers and cooks and bakers. 14 He will take the best of your fields and vineyards and olive groves and give them to his attendants. 15 He will take a tenth of your grain and of your vintage and give it to his officials and attendants. 16 Your menservants and maidservants and the best of your cattle and donkeys he will take for his own use. 17 He will take a tenth of your flocks, and you yourselves will become his slaves. 18 When

*that day comes, you will cry out for relief from the king you
have chosen, and the Lord will not answer you in that day."*

*19 But the people refused to listen to Samuel. "No!"
they said. "We want a king over us. 20 Then we will
be like all the other nations, with a king to lead us
and to go out before us and fight our battles."*

1 Sam 8:4-20

As Samuel approached God with the people's demand for a
king like everybody else, God told him that by the people's request,
they have not rejected him, Samuel, but they have reject Him. He
went on to list the abuse that was going to come on them and their
entire nation which included individuals, their children and their
economy. Rejection of the word of God (His instructions to us, His
desires, plans and purposes) leaves us exposed to abuse. God and His
word are one and the same; He is His word and His word is Him.
Therefore rejecting His word means that we are rejecting Him and
His rule as rule as king over our lives as the people of Israel did. We
must understand what we are giving up when we reject God.

The Apostle Paul said those who walk in the flesh (an enemy of
God) and does not submit to His rule, cannot inherit the kingdom.
Being in the Kingdom of God means having Him as our king and
living in all the benefits of His kingdom. The Greek word for "walk"
as used in Galatians 5:16, is peripateo and one of its meaning is "to
be occupied with" which means to live or to focus on. If we are
occupied with satisfying our flesh we cannot enjoy the benefits of the
Kingdom of God. David outlines clearly in Psalms 91, the benefits
of us living and remaining in God:

*He who dwells in the secret place of the Most High
shall abide under the shadow of the Almighty.*

Ps 91:1

To dwell in the secret place of the Most High is to accept and adhere to His commands and to submit to His rule. When we do this we will abide (remain, live, rest) under His shadow which means we are able to enjoy the benefits of His kingship:

- Protection
- Deliverance
- Health
- Rest
- Peace of mind
- Victory
- Prosperity
- Angelic support
- Long life

All who dwell in a king's domain are his responsibility and are sheltered by the canopy of his presence. It therefore means, that anything or anyone who tries to come against you to harm you must first overcome the one casting the shadow who in this case is the King of Glory. Since He is the Lord of Host, the Lord Mighty in battle, we know that we are already victorious over our enemies. To remove oneself from the protection and provision of God through disobedience and rejection of His word means vulnerability to the enemy's attacks.

Rejecting God means forfeiting our rights to all of the accompanying benefits and leaving ourselves exposed to abuse.

Not a Bargain

*(In this case study, the names have been changed
to protect the identities of persons)*

The night appeared darker than usual. The sight of her own blood sent shivers through her body and further intensified her heart break. Disappointed was by far an understatement of the emotional state Dominique was in. As she lay in bed recalling the evening's occurrence, she was almost numb to her physical pain as the excruciating pain of her breaking heart surpassed that of her bruises. She remembered the look in his eyes just before the first blow struck. It had taken a while for it to register to her that he had hit her. Even now, tears welled up in her eyes as she recalled the scene.

"How can a man who loved me so much come to hate me so much? How can he look at me and hit me?" she asked herself. She had always heard that Mark had a bad temper and was always getting into fights. There were even times before they were married when they would get into arguments and he would get into fights with others. "But his temper was never targeted at me" she thought, "He was always so gently with me."

She recalled times when the Holy Spirit would prompt her to leave the relationship while they were still courting. There were also church leaders who advised her of the dangers of continuing under such circumstances. But Dominique felt she knew him better than anyone. The deeper she got into the relationship with Mark, the more her relationship with God suffered. She had seen and known personally of other abuse cases and vowed that she would never allow it to happen to her. Now here she was; the object of abuse in her marriage and thinking "when did this become me? How did this become me?"

Profile of an Abuser

[vi]Let me first point out that an abuser does not become an abuser over night. There are a number of contributing factors to a person reaching the place of abusing another. If observed carefully, one would notice that there are numerous signs exhibited over a period by a potential abuser. However, quite often these signs are overlooked by those closest to them particularly the one subject to the abuse; as in the case of Dominique and Mark. Ignoring or pretending the signs are not there, would not make them disappear nor does it cause the person to change. Too many persons are gambling their lives away, by seeing the signs and ignoring them. Some have even experienced abuse prior to marriage, yet they go ahead and enter the marriage with that person in hopes that the abuser would change in the process of being married. Signs give indication of what is ahead: if the signs along the road say "Abuse Ahead'" rest assured that's where you will end up if you remain on that road. There are some distinguishing attitudes and behaviors which are characteristic of an abuser or potential abuser. [vii]Some of these include:

- He or she is frequently short tempered—it does not take much for them to get angry (they are often easily insulted)
- Excessively jealous—may go as far as accusing the victim of perceived affairs. They usually also keep track of their victim; never trusting to leave them in the company of others for fear of what they may reveal.
- Tries to isolate the victim from other relationships that may serve as a source of support e.g. friends, family, church, social activities.
- Insecure—these persons are often insecure and have a low self esteem, hence the need to feel in control of the victim. They may try to belittle the victim in an attempt to build their own self image.

- They do not take responsibility for their own actions; they blame others for the way they feel, the way they think and the things they do. In their minds, someone else always made them do it. You would hear them making such statements like "you made me angry", "you made me do it", "if you would do what I say, I would not have had to hurt you". They play on the sympathy of the victim.
- In many cases, they may have a history of violence.
- They may tend to be cruel to others including children, animals, and even themselves.
- Some may have a fascination with weapons
- In many cases they are found to force their victims to have sex with them against their will
- Many of them are unfaithful to their partners and in some cases accuse their partners of being the unfaithful ones. Proverbs 13:2 says ". . . . the unfaithful have a craving for violence.

If you know someone who is displaying these characteristics, that individual needs immediate help. These signs should not be overlooked. Such a person would need to speak to a counselor as soon as possible.

Profile of a Victim

Many abuse victims are found to display some similar characteristics. In many instances, these very characteristics give greater insight into the victim's reasons for remaining with the abuser and in so doing permit the abuse to continue. [viii]Persons who are victims of abuse in relationships usually display the following characteristics:

- Low self esteem
- Financial dependency

- A great need to be loved and accepted
- Are usually stressed and may complain of stress related conditions /illnesses such as headaches, stomach pains, frequent irregular menstrual cycle etc.
- Depression
- Accepts blame and guilt for the abuse done to them
- Often makes excuses and defends the abuser's behavior
- Always believes the abuser will change
- Isolated from friends and family
- Considers leaving or may have left the relationship but keeps returning.

Many of these people have lost their sense of self worth and believe that this is the best they can do. The mistake many persons around them make is to desert them because of anger toward them for remaining in the relationship. What we don't realize is that they need a friend more than ever. Turning our backs on them is exactly what the abuser wants; isolation of their victim. They need to know that there is someone there for them to speak to and turn to at any time. The victims who succumb to isolation from family and friends eventually lose their lives.

Chapter Highlights

- There are no justifiable reasons for abuse.
- Abuse is manipulative, self seeking and is likened unto witchcraft.
- When we set out to manipulate a person, we are setting ourselves up as that person's sovereign authority which is in direct opposition/rebellion to the authority of God.
- All who dwell in a king's domain are his responsibility and are sheltered by the canopy of his presence.
- To remove one's self from the protection and provision of God through disobedience and rejection of His word means vulnerability to the enemy's attack
- An abuser does not become an abuser over night.
- Victims of abuse need to know that there is someone there for them at any given time.

Chapter Nine

The Seed of Abuse

In Hebrews 11:3, we are told that the things we see were not made from things we see but rather from the things that we do not see. Abuse that we see outworked did not begin with the manifestation that we see displayed but rather with what we do not see. We have been looking at the psychological aspects of abuse but at this time we are going to look at the spiritual reality of abuse which is the greater reality. All that we see around us are reflection and manifestation of the occurrences in the spirit realm. Ephesians 6:12 says that we are not fighting against flesh and blood (physical) but against principalities, powers, rulers of the darkness of this world, spiritual wickedness in high places (spiritual enemy). Thus, the battle requires spiritual weapons.

Many abusers, as well as victims, have unconsciously been sucked into a cycle of abuse. Many of victims of the abuse cases I have encountered attested that a parent, grandparent or even great grandparent was abusive and as a result they (the victims) have become abusers themselves. Have you ever met anyone who has witnessed the abused of a parent, friend or have been abused themselves and since they could empathize with it, they vowed never to do it to anyone? Yet, they find themselves doing the same thing they vowed never to do. What has happened? Or what about a young girl who has witnessed her mom being abused by her father, and vowed never to get married to someone like him. Eventually, she marries a man who abuses her. What went wrong?

Actually, none of these persons in themselves might have intended to get caught in the web of abuse. As a matter of fact, many of them are surprised and disappointed in themselves for getting caught in the very same thing they were running from. What are the reasons for such happenings?

This is what has happened: a seed of abuse was deposited into their lives unknowing to them and often times, unknowing to those who sow the seed (persons in the abuse situation through whom the devil worked). This seed is usually deposited during their childhood years. It was about one year ago, the Holy Spirit dropped this in my spirit. I was really taken aback and now that I am sharing on this issue it has been brought back to my memory. If we grasp this, it would change how we approach our relationships with spouses, children and leadership approaches in the Body of Christ. It would cause us to revisit the foundation of our relationships to ensure that there is nothing there which the enemy can use as an access point to our lives and relationships.

Many persons in this busy, self absorbed world take childhood for granted. Many parents have become caught up in going after every opportunity that presents itself; working two or three jobs to gain the things that honestly will not last. Some are trying to secure a romantic relationship because of some benefit which they feel it will provide, whether financially or sexually. Sadly, all of this is done at the expense of their children.

Childhood years are vital to the development and success of any individual. Research has shown that a fetus is able to respond to its external environment as early as nine weeks of pregnancy. It has also been found after birth, the new babies are able to recognize the voice of their mother and even songs that might have been sung to them while they were still in the womb. I remembered when I was pregnant with my daughter I loved listening to music and singing. During the final two months of my pregnancy, I would worship and dance with my all; at times forgetting I was pregnant. After she was born, one of the only way we were able to calm her quickly was through music. My husband used to play the trumpet while she was asleep and she would continue sleeping soundly. We concluded that obviously she had learned and recognized all of these from her time in the womb.

It is believed that whatever, we teach a child during the first five years of their lives helps to forge their identity. The Bible says that we must train up our children in the way they should go and when they are older they will not depart from it. We need to seize the formative years by sowing godly principles into their minds which in turn influence who they become. A child's or rather a person's personality is greatly influenced by what he or she is taught whether through what they hear, what they see demonstrated before them or what they experienced. These are the 'seeds' to which I refer. Each seed has within itself the potential for growth and multiplication, thus producing certain characteristics in keeping with the nature of the seed sown. For example, if you plant a mango seed, in time a mango tree will grow and bear mangoes providing it receives the necessary nourishment and right atmosphere needed for growth. Should these conditions be met, that seed will germinate, grow into a mature tree and bear fruits containing seeds with the same potential to produce other trees and fruits of its kind.

We must understand that the devil is seeking to take advantage of the formative years of children because the perception is if he seizes the child, he possesses the adult, which is what we are supposed to be doing for the kingdom of God. When a child is surrounded by and experiences abuse, that seed of abuse is sown into that child's life. Quite often it may lie dormant for years and is released in time particularly when the right conditions are met. Satan hates humanity and desires to destroy us. Jesus says this about him:

> *The thief comes only in order to steal and kill and*
> *destroy. I came that they may have and enjoy life, and*
> *have it in abundance (to the full, till it overflows).*

John 10:10

Let us consider the young woman who has seen her father abuse her mother; she hates the situation and has vowed never to marry anyone like her father but then she realized that she has married an abuser. From her childhood a seed of abuse was sown into her life. The enemy knows she has been exposed to abuse and its seed has been deposited. He also knows that it requires the right conditions to manifest which he intends to accommodate. Unless she comes to the place of surrendering totally to Christ by submitting daily to the authority of His word those abusive tendencies, eventually would begin to operate in her. Remember, the spiritual reality is more real than the seen/manifested reality. That seed of abuse in her attracts the necessary conditions for it to grow and bear fruits: the enemy would begin to work on his destructive plan by setting his agent in place (the spirit behind the abuser) to facilitate the seed growing. Bear in mind that his goal is to steal, kill and to destroy. I have come to realize that abusers are not usually attracted to anyone and everyone. There are certain persons with whom an abuser would never get involved. There is a saying "monkey knows which limb to swing on". An abuser would never stick around a person with a strong personality who is confident in who they are. Instead, he would attach himself to a person who has some vulnerability to his attacks. That seed must be recognized and dealt with. Jesus said that He came to give life and to give it in abundance; without lack. Deliverance from the seed of abuse can only come through submission to Christ and obedience to His words which is spirit and life:

> *The Spirit gives life; the flesh counts for nothing. The words I have spoken to you are spirit and they are life.*

John 6:63

In Matthew 18: 23-35, we read of a certain unmerciful servant who after being forgiven of his debt by his master, went out and threw his brother in jail for owing him far less than the amount for which he was indebted. This news of his inconsistency reached his master and he had him thrown to the tormentors. Torment means the act of harassing someone, to treat cruelly, subject to torture, in other words to be abused. An atmosphere of unforgiveness contributes to the right conditions for the seed of abuse to grow and flourish in your life. Imagine living with or being in the presence of someone who is unforgiving. Such a person would emanate with anger, malice and bitterness. The atmosphere he or she creates is a very unhappy one and everyone within that sphere is likely to experience the effects of it. Unforgiveness strips you and those in your home/surrounding of peace, joy and freedom. When you have been wronged, forgive and do so quickly because it opens the way for you to enjoy peace of mind and live a full and happy life.

Chapter Highlights

- Childhood years are vital to the development and success of any individual.
- We need to seize the formative years of our children by sowing Godly principles into their lives which in turn influence who they become.
- Each seed has within itself the potential for growth and multiplication, thus producing certain characteristics in keeping with the nature of the seed sown.
- When a child is surrounded by and experiences abuse, that seed of abuse is being sown into that child.
- Deliverance from the seed of abuse can only come through submission to Christ and obedience to his words which is spirit and life
- An atmosphere of unforgiveness contributes to the right conditions for the seed of abuse to grow and flourish in ones life.

CHAPTER TEN

TYPES OF ABUSE

Abuse occurs at many levels and in every area where we find relationships[9] in our world. From the baby in his mother's womb to the work place and it even spills over to the church. There are many expert authorities who are highly qualified in this subject area and I do applaud them for their skilled analysis. In this chapter, we will be looking at some of the most common types of abuse which occur in the home since this makes it easier to be able to identify and put steps in place to stop or prevent them all together.

Domestic Abuse

As the name suggests, domestic abuse occurs in the home. It is not limited to any particular class, ethnic or religious group. Generally, domestic abuse involves any form of cruelty, control, violence exerted in a relationship by one party on another which takes place in the home setting. Whenever, we think about domestic abuse, we usually instantaneously associate it with physical abuse where a lover, usually a husband or wife (yes wife) kicks or slaps the other person which is only partly correct. Physical abuse is only one form of domestic abuse. There are different forms of domestic abuse and it is important that we identify these because many persons may be living with it and thinks that it is normal relational behavior since they are not being physically abused. Some statistics has shown

---

9   A relationship is any connection between two or more entities whether emotionally or other (paraphrased)

that one out of every two marriages is experiencing some form of domestic abuse. If the statistics are true, it therefore means that half or more of the marriages in the church are experiencing the same. Ignorance is to be credited for this imprisonment linked to abuse. In Hosea 4:6 God says.

> *my people are destroyed from lack of knowledge*
> ***(ignorance).*** (emphasis added)

Jesus puts it this way in John 8:32:

> *. . . . And you will know the truth, and*
> *the truth will set you free."*

Note carefully that Jesus did not just say that the truth shall set you free; he said you shall know the truth. To know in the Greek context actually means to become acquainted with, to learn, to come to know, to perceive or to understand. This implies that the knowledge of truth goes beyond just hearing it or simply being aware of it but to be knowledgeable requires action and allowing it to take effect in one's life. In other words, it is your knowledge of the truth that will set free while ignorance of the truth keeps you in captivity. If you are desirous of walking in freedom, you must make a conscious effort/take action to know truth. It is in our best interest to be armed with truth so we can send abuse packing when it raises its ugly head. We will look at a few forms of abuse which are common in the home.

- **Physical Abuse**—this form of abuse is characterized by physical violence which entails one person punching, kicking, slapping and carrying out other acts of violence against the other person. This is usually done by the abuser in an attempt to subdue the other person bringing them under their control. It is appalling how many persons in society are living with physical abuse and even more devastating is the number of persons who have died as a result of it. Quite often where there is abuse in a relationship, it began with some other form of abuse usually verbal and emotional/psychological abuse.

- **Emotional/Psychological Abuse**—This usually entails threats being made by the abuser to the victim in order to control them. This strategy is a direct attack on the mind of the victim. The mental condition of a person affects his entire well being. The aim is to influence the thought pattern of the person. The primary tool used to accomplish this is words. Words are very powerful; they can either create or destroy. These victims usually have a low self image and are very receptive to the words and threats directed at them from their abuser. These words define them and create the universe in which they live. Words have the ability to give life or cause death. They can set you free or hold you captive. We are cautioned in Colossians 2:8, not to let anyone hold us captive (imprison, box in, lock in a small place, limit your growth or advancement) through the words they teach. Leaders must realize that there is a difference between motivation and manipulation. Motivation employs truth/principles from the Word of God to encourage transformation in the lives of the people being led and brings them to the place of operating in their full potential. The methods used are fueled by genuine love and concern for the individual. Manipulation, on the other hand, employs means of deception/falsehood in order to get a person to do what the leader wants them to do even if it is to their detriment. The primary aim of manipulation is to complete a task by any means necessary. Manipulation impedes the growth of the people being led while motivation promotes growth. To manipulate people is to abuse them psychologically. In order to avoid emotionally abusing the people, leaders must be careful to teach them the truth of God's word. Persons who are being emotionally abused may find themselves being stressed, depressed, unhappy, suicidal and suffering from stress related disorders such as frequent headaches, stomach and abdominal cramps, ulcers, loss of appetite, overeating, irregular periods, and constipation. Another means by which psychological abuse can be inflicted is by withholding ones speech 'the silent treatment'. We have heard that actions speak louder than words; a person may choose to be silent but their attitudes and behavior give a clear indication of their every thought. Unspoken words or 'the silent treatment' can be very hostile. In a marriage, a spouse may choose to withhold his or her speech as a means of starving the other of their need for conversation. They may view it as a way to discipline their spouse for something that was done or not done or an unfulfilled expectation. Such an act is cruel and malicious. Malice is defined in the Merriam Webster Dictionary as a desire to cause pain, injury or distress to another. If the motive behind the silence is to cause distress and suffering, it is malicious and according to Galatians 5:21, those who practice this will not inherit the Kingdom of God.

- **Verbal Abuse**—this form of abuse is very common in society. It is where the abuser continually insults the victim thus damaging their self image, self confidence and generally belittles them. It negatively/incorrectly defines the person using such statements like "you are fat", "you are stupid", "You are ugly", "you will never become anything" and more. It is not the true definition for the person but because of the insecurity that's already there, the victim accepts it as true. When I speak of insults, I am also referring to any form of derogatory statements made to someone which would inflict pain. It must be taken into consideration that the definition of insult may vary based on the individual for what one person may consider an insult may be a joke for someone else. Meanwhile, what may break one person, may build another. This is why in relationships; time must be taken to know each other: their likes and dislikes, strengths and weaknesses, confidence and insecurities. Each party should endeavor to see each other grow. Of course the need may arise for constructive criticism in building a stronger relationship but all must be done in love.

- **Sexual Abuse**—This is the one most of us are knowledgeable of. It includes all forms of sexual violence: rape, forced sex within marriage, rough sex etc. Like the other forms of abuse we have looked at, its aim is to control the victim. Sexual abuse is a selfish act and has nothing to do with love.

- **Child Abuse**—this one I have summed up as any form of abuse that is meted out to a child such as physical, emotional, and sexual. Almost every day we hear of children who are beaten, raped, and molested by some adult whether it is a parent, teacher, family member, friend or religious leader. Although many such cases have been exposed, there is still a great percentage that is shrouded by secrecy. Many of these children are defenseless and scared and some because of threats are forced to remain silent. This is displeasing to God! It is a strategy formulated at the gates of hell against the future of our nations. The intention is to infiltrate the minds of the children and in the process damage the lives of our future generation. But Glory to God, we have the promise of Christ which is our defense.

18 . . . . and upon this rock I will build my church;
and the gates of hell shall not prevail against it.

Matt 16:18

We need to fervently advance the Kingdom of God, by making disciples of all nations as Jesus commanded us, and we do this by teaching them to obey all that Christ commanded; teach them the principles, the laws and the culture of the Kingdom of God beginning with our children.

Chapter Highlights

- Domestic abuse involves any form of cruelty, control, violence exerted in a relationship by one party on another which takes place in the home setting.
- Words are very powerful; they can either create or destroy.
- Apart from verbal abuse being emotionally abusive, giving the 'silent treatment' can be really detrimental because it starves the other party of meaningful conversation.

Chapter Eleven

Disarming the Abuser

For there to be an abuse equation, there are two main components which must be in place:

Abuser (the giver) + Victim (the recipient) = ABUSE

If we remove the victim/recipient from the equation, the abuse process is incomplete and is, therefore, ineffective.

One of the primary ways of disarming the abuser is by removing the victim from the equation. I am not saying to take the victim and send them to some far away land, although in some extreme cases this may be considered an option. Rather, I am speaking of empowering or arming them to change their status as victims. You would recall in chapter eight, that we had established that abusers do not generally attach themselves to any and everyone but primarily to potential victims. They operate like predators seeking a prey and a wounded prey is much easier to control. The question therefore is: how do we arm victims to change their status? I have made a few suggestions below of how this can be accomplished:

1. By encouraging them to seek counseling—if you are a victim of abuse or know someone who is, I strongly recommend counseling and being a child of God, I would say not just any counseling but Christian counseling. Christian counseling sessions should be done under the guidance of the Holy Spirit. Thus, the root causes of abuse can be unearthed allowing true healing to take place. The victim is brought to a place where he or she can identify the problem and decide upon the best course of action. They are able to

express themselves freely, emptying themselves of all bottled up emotions, unexpressed thoughts, fears and hurts which consequently prepare them to receive and embrace new life.

2. Previously, we identified certain characteristics which are common among abuse victims such as low self esteem, low self image, a great need to be loved and accepted at any cost. These are indications that he or she is ignorant of their true value and purpose; who they are, why they exist and whose they are. The person who is ignorant of their true purpose in life is vulnerable to abuse (being abnormally used). Such a person needs to become infused with the true knowledge of who they are. Proverbs 24:5 says *"The wise are mightier than the strong, and those with knowledge grow stronger and stronger."* Their pattern of thinking needs to change from one of victim to victor. If you think like a victim you will operate like a victim. Likewise, if you think like a victor you will operate like one. Romans 12:2 tells us that we are transformed as our minds are renewed and our minds are renewed as we understand and apply the truth of God's word. This is when the true identity of the person, as created by God, is revealed. The identity of victim which the person would have previously embraced was a pseudo/false identity which must be done away with. If they are to truly live a victorious life, they must come into their true identity which is only found in Christ Jesus.

3. They must become financially empowered—one of the reasons why many people, particularly women remain in abusive relationships is because they are financially dependent on the abuser. I encourage women who are in such a position to seek employment. Even if you have not completed school for whatever reason, you are not void of potential. God created you and placed gifts and talents inside of you. There is something you can do! Cook, sew, or write your way to freedom! You do have something in your

hands you can work with and whatever He has given to you, have the capacity to generate wealth for you.

A gift opens the way for the giver and ushers
him into the presence of the great.

Prov 18:16

The abuser is also disarmed when the victim brings awareness to the abuse whether it is to a pastor, friend, elder or the police. How often have we met women who have been physically abused and chose to remain silent? She may not want anyone to know because she is ashamed or afraid of what persons would say or view her if they find out; so she puts on dark sunglasses, concealer or gives explanations for her bruises. By remaining silent and covering it up, she is actually strengthening her abuser. I once heard a woman say, if her husband should ever hit her, she would never cover up any bruises nor conceal any black eye but she would go to work, church and everywhere else just as she is. When she said this we all laughed but it was very serious. Such an act on her part would be a strong statement against abuse and it would bring awareness (light) into the situation. Secrecy is equivalent to darkness and the enemy thrives on darkness. The entry of light into the situation, like the sunrise, signals newness, freshness, change, hope and life.

Another way of disarming the abuser is by forgiving them. I know that at the mention of this word "forgive" the lawyer in many would leap to his or her feet exclaiming "I object Your Honor". Although we may want to argue vehemently on why it is so difficult to forgive; it is imperative for us to do so if we are to break the yoke of abuse from off our lives.

In the next chapter we will take a closer look at this whole aspect of forgiveness. Someone once said that the person who angers you actually controls you. Have you ever had someone hurt you and as an act of revenge you refuse to let go and you feel the urge to hate them? You may think that the less you speak to them, is the more it would hurt them. Wrong; actually, the person who is being damaged the most is you. I recall Joyce Meyer making a powerful statement which stuck with me. She said "unforgiveness is like drinking poison and expecting the other person to die". The person who is being destroyed by unforgiveness is the person carrying it around. There are a lot of persons who have been abused or deeply hurt and have broken free physically in that they are no longer in the situation but whenever they hear the name, think about or see the person, deep anger and hatred wells up in them as fresh as the day the hurt occurred. Sadly, they have not truly broken free from their abuse and wherever unforgiveness is reigning, torment is inevitable.

14 "If you forgive those who sin against you, your heavenly Father will forgive you. 15 But if you refuse to forgive others, your Father will not forgive your sins.

Matt 6:14-15

34 In anger his master turned him over to the jailers to be tortured, until he should pay back all he owed.

35 "This is how my heavenly Father will treat each of you unless you forgive your brother from your heart."

Matt 18:34-35

Forgiveness releases you to walk in freedom and empowers you to move forward and live a productive and successful life.

Chapter Highlights

- In removing the victim from the abuse equation, they must be empowered or armed to change their status as victim.
- In counseling the victims are able to express themselves freely, emptying themselves of all bottled up emotions, unexpressed thoughts, fears and hurts which consequently prepare them to receive and embrace new life.
- The person who is ignorant of their true purpose in life is vulnerable to abuse
- If we are to truly live a victorious life, we must come into our true identity which is only found in Christ Jesus.
- Secrecy is equivalent to darkness and the enemy thrives on darkness.
- The entry of light into the situation, like the sunrise, signals newness, freshness, change, hope and life.
- Forgiveness releases you to walk in freedom and empowers you to move forward and live a productive and successful life.
- wherever unforgiveness is reigning, torment is inevitable

CHAPTER TWELVE

FORGIVE TO LIVE

Forgiveness does not mean forgetting. The truth is you may never forget the wrong that was done to you. It is a choice made in obedience to God; releasing the person for the wrong they have done to you. When you choose to forgive, you are saying "yes Lord, not my will but yours be done". It is His Spirit that then empowers us to carry it out. It is a sure act of faith and obedience. If we are to determine forgiveness by the way we feel about a person, we may never feel the need to forgive. Bear in mind that the flesh is always fighting against what the Spirit wants. It always wants to do its own thing and have its own way. This is why we are told in Colossians 3:5 "to put our evil desires (the flesh) to death" because it tries to rebel against the authority of God. Our carnal mind will always want to argue and try to justify itself and its actions. It is possible for you to feel all the wrong things but choose to do what is right.

You might be saying "but that's not an easy thing to do". And I do agree with you; it is not easy to yield to the will of God. Jesus was faced with such a decision.

> 39 Jesus went out as usual to the Mount of Olives, and his
> disciples followed him. 40 On reaching the place, he said
> to them, "Pray that you will not fall into temptation." 41
> He withdrew about a stone's throw beyond them, knelt
> down and prayed, 42 "Father, if you are willing, take this
> cup from me; yet not my will, but yours be done." 43 An
> angel from heaven appeared to him and strengthened him.
> 44 And being in anguish, he prayed more earnestly, and
> his sweat was like drops of blood falling to the ground.

Luke 22:39-44

Jesus' choice was not an easy one. This was a very difficult time for him since he was about to soon suffer much for all of mankind and there was a major struggle between his flesh and the Spirit. So deeply agonizing was this moment for him that the author told us his sweat was like blood; yet he made a decision to exalt the will of God above his own. The moment he made such a decision and confessed it, an angel appeared and strengthened him. He was empowered to execute the will and purpose of God to whom he had chosen to yield. It is imperative that we understand that God releases what we need in the time we need it as we yield to His will. We, in the church, must learn to follow His instructions as He issues them. Further instructions will not be given until we obey those that were already given. When you choose to subdue your flesh and forgive despite of your feelings, the Spirit of God will empower you to carry it out.

. . . . 'Not by might nor by power, but by My Spirit,'
Says the Lord of hosts.

Zech 4:6

I had never understood or thought it necessary for the Spirit to help me as it relates to forgiving someone. You see, I had struggled with unforgiveness for years because I thought it was mine to perform entirely. I thought I had to change my feelings, get rid of my hurts, feel love towards the persons and forget the situation all by myself. Well it seemed to work for a while. I had convinced myself that I had really forgiven those who had hurt me but what I had actually done was suppress my anger.

For those of you struggling with forgiving someone right now, I want you to know that it is possible for you to be free to do it. It would be very easy for me to speak at you; telling you what you must do or what you are expected to do but I feel the need to give testimony, bear witness, give evidence to the fact that Jesus Christ is real and he is still able to deliver you from unforgiveness. He is very much concerned about every area of your life. You may have been hurt over and over again, used and abused by people including spouse, parents, friends and even those in the church and you may say that you are tired and want nothing to do with anyone or the church. I was very active in church: saved for years, a worship leader, ministry dancer, responsible for the dance and drama team. Interestingly, I was being smothered under the weight of unforgiveness. In the presence of everyone, I would appear fine but when I was alone, I would feel like my air passage was being blocked by all the hurts and pains. As a matter of fact, I used to suffer from frequent shortness of breath although I was not an asthmatic case. Unforgiveness had journeyed with me from childhood and instead of getting better, it seemed like I had become a greater magnet for hurts and with each hurt it became more difficult to forgive. Although I was saved and had been for years, my spiritual growth was greatly impeded. I felt like I was besieged by the spirits of anger, bitterness, hatred, unforgiveness and malice as the hurts came from all directions. It continued for years until I came to the realization that I was losing my relationship with God. I had stopped going to fellowship; I would cry continually and was having frequent outburst of anger. I remember seeing myself in a dark room with an open door ahead with a bright light in it. The more I reached for it, the further I felt myself being soaked away. I decided at that point that I could not afford to lose my relationship with God so I cried out for help. He then ministered to me that the Holy Spirit was there to help and empower me to do anything even to forgive. I had never thought of asking Him to help me to forgive; I had always seen it as my sole responsibility. At that moment my deliverance began. I wish I could tell you that immediately all the hurts went away and that I loved everyone immediately but I cannot. It began the process for me and as I continued to yield to the Spirit's rule in my life, the more the fruit of love was manifested. The more I obeyed the word of God, the more it healed and transformed me. Eventually, I was able to see those persons and not even remember the acts of hurts unless I did so deliberately. As I chose to forgive,

God's love, joy and peace just flooded my life. It does not mean that difficulties and hurtful situations did not present themselves after that. Every time those difficult and trying times came they were growth opportunities for me to overcome unforgiveness. They were trials to train me to be able to manage what God had and have in store for me but at the time I was failing because I chose to hold on to the pain. In order for you to receive what God is giving to you (freedom, peace, joy and more) you have to open your hands and release that which you are holding on to (hurts, pain, unforgiveness). We cannot fathom God; Isaiah 55:8-9 says His ways are above our ways and His thoughts above our thoughts:

> 8 *"For my thoughts are not your thoughts,*
> *neither are your ways my ways,"*
> *declares the Lord.*

> 9 *"As the heavens are higher than the earth,*
> *so are my ways higher than your ways*
> *and my thoughts than your thoughts.*

> **Isa 55:8-9**

We need to trust in the omniscience and wisdom of God and his unfailing love for us. We will not always understand His methods but know that He intends it for our good. Who would have thought that God by drawing satan's attention to Job was actually initiating a process that was going to prepare him, Job, for blessing which he had not even request.

> *6 Now there was a day when the sons of God came to present themselves before the Lord, and Satan also came among them.*

> *7 And the Lord said to Satan, "From where do you come?" So Satan answered the Lord and said, "From going to and fro on the earth, and from walking back and forth on it."*

8 Then the Lord said to Satan, "Have you considered My servant Job, that there is none like him on the earth, a blameless and upright man, one who fears God and shuns evil?"

Job 1:6-8

We might look at Job's trial and think that was a very hard thing to do but Job's trial prepared him for what was about to be released. In the end he had to say this after God had revealed His omnipotence to him like never before:

Then Job answered the Lord and said:

*2 "I know that You can do everything,
And that no purpose of Yours can be withheld from You.*

*3 You asked, 'Who is this who hides
counsel without knowledge?'
Therefore I have uttered what I did not understand,
Things too wonderful for me, which I did not know.*

*4 Listen, please, and let me speak;
You said, 'I will question you, and you shall answer Me.'*

*5 "I have heard of You by the hearing of the ear,
But now my eye sees You.*

Job 42:1-5

What an awesome God we serve! There is nothing too hard for Him. By yourself it may seem impossible to forgive your abuser or abusers but with Christ you can do all things.

Chapter Highlights

- Forgiving the person for the wrong they have done to you is a choice.
- When you choose to subdue your flesh and forgive despite of your feelings, the Spirit of God will empower you to carry it out.
- In order for you to receive what God is giving to you (freedom, peace, joy and more) you have to open your hands and release that which you are holding on to (hurts, pain, unforgiveness).

Chapter Thirteen

Word to the Abuser

The title of this chapter may imply that I will proceed to hammer the abusive man or woman into the ground for his or her abusive tendencies. Well I am afraid I would have to disappoint you because that is not what it is about. It is in our nature as human beings to quickly see the speck in our neighbor's eye but not notice the plank that is in ours. We are often quick to see someone else's wrong and what they need to do to fix it but we are usually the last to see when something is wrong with us. Quite a few of us if not more, would have exhibited some abusive tendency towards someone at one time or other whether it would have been physically, financially, emotionally, verbally, you name it. In whatever way, in whatever measure, abuse is abuse!

Generally, women are viewed as the ones more likely to be victims while men on the other hand because of their rough exterior and often aggressive nature are usually considered and presumed to be the abuser. However, recent statistics have revealed that there are many men who are victims of verbal and emotional abuse. It is not easy to admit this since I am a woman of many words and usually have to make a conscious effort to put a bridle on my tongue. We would scarcely find a man reporting a case of abuse or speaking of it because everyone including him does not expect men to be victims. We think he should be strong, impenetrable, in control and for him to admit victimization would mean weakness and disrespect. So to maintain his masculine image, he chooses to internalize his feelings and suffer in silence which may prove dangerous because one day he may lose control and hurt someone which more than likely may be his abuser, the woman. So an abuser does not have a class, a particular look or gender. It can be anyone.

To the person or persons who find that they have been inflicting abuse on others, I want you to know that God loves you with an unfailing love.

> *22 Through the Lord's mercies we are not consumed,*
> *Because His compassions fail not.*
>
> *23 They are new every morning;*
> *Great is Your faithfulness.*

Lam 3:22-23

The Message version puts it this way:

> *22 God's loyal love couldn't have run out,*
> *his merciful love couldn't have dried up.*
>
> *23 They're created new every morning.*
> *How great your faithfulness!*

Lam 3:22-23

He hates your abusive ways (the sin) but He loves you. Jesus Christ died and rose again so you can be set free. God did not create you to be an abuser: In Jeremiah 29:11, He says this

> *I know the plans that I have for you, declares the*
> *Lord. They are plans for peace and not disaster,*
> *plans to give you a future filled with hope.*

Jer 29:11

You probably never intended or desired to abuse anyone. At one time in your life, you might have been a victim of abuse; you hated it but now you find yourself doing it to others: your children, your husband, your wife, yourself. You might have been labeled an abuser. You may be disgusted with your actions and have disqualified yourself from becoming anyone better in life. The place you find yourself is an exile, a hard place, a dry place, fruitless, unproductive and a lifeless place to you. But God has a plan which is outlined in this manner:

> *13 When you look for me, you will find me. When you wholeheartedly seek me, 14 I will let you find me, declares the Lord. I will bring you back from captivity. I will gather you from all the nations and places where I've scattered you, declares the Lord. I will bring you back from the place where you are being held captive.*

Jer 29:13-14

Now that you have read this, you are now on divine appointment and this is your time for deliverance. The Spirit of the Lord is drawing you into a whole new life, a free life, an abundant life. Jesus came to set the captives free and you qualify for freedom. If you are tired of the devil using you as his tool to carry out abuse and fulfill his plan to steal, kill and destroy please pray these words:

Lord, I am tired of the way I have been living. I am tired of hurting myself and others. I confess that I have been wrong. I have sinned against you. Jesus, be my Lord; set me free. I forgive all those who have ever hurt me. Lord let Your love full my heart now; change me for Your glory. Amen.

CHAPTER FOURTEEN

PUTTING IT ALL TOGETHER

Unless the Lord builds the house,
its builders labor in vain.
Unless the Lord watches over the city,
the watchmen stand guard in vain.

Ps 127:1

A relationship is a work in progress. Like a building under construction, it takes time, effort and dedication. For any structure to be correctly built there needs to be continuous reference to the blueprint of the structure. If we are going to receive the maximum rewards and productivity from our relationships with spouses, children, work, and church we have to build accurate relationships and for the relationship to be accurate it must be according to God's design: His blueprint which is His word.

David said unless God builds the house, we are wasting our time doing it on our own. I see the relational issues mentioned in this book as cracks in the structure which weakens it. I pray that as we have addressed these subject areas in view of the word of God, that you will re-evaluated your relationships, identify the cracks and be willing and ready to make the required changes according to the word of God. It is not enough to hear or read the Bible but there must be application of the principles given. This is how your understanding/belief is validated. This is what Jesus said:

24 "Therefore everyone who hears these words of mine and
puts them into practice is like a wise man who built his house

*on the rock. 25 The rain came down, the streams rose, and
the winds blew and beat against that house; yet it did not fall,
because it had its foundation on the rock. 26 But everyone
who hears these words of mine and does not put them into
practice is like a foolish man who built his house on sand. 27
The rain came down, the streams rose, and the winds blew
and beat against that house, and it fell with a great crash."*

Matt 7:24-27

Obedience is the key. God desires to prosper you. As a matter of
fact, He has already blessed you with all spiritual blessing in heavenly
places in Christ (Eph. 1:3) but it is your faith demonstrated by your
acts of obedience that will cause them to materialize in the physical.
You are in a new day and a new dimension has been opened to you.
I believe and declare that your life and your family will not be the
same. I declare in the name of Jesus that your worst is behind you,
your today is greater than yesterday and your best is yet to come.

APPENDIX

Discussion Starters

True to life scenarios to encourage discussions in your women's group, men's group and even youth group. (All characters named are not linked to any known individual)

Scenario One:

Desmond and Cindy are two young people who are about to get married in two months. They have been courting for three years and believe that they are ready for marriage because they love each other. They love and fear God and they have a lot in common. They do have one major concern however: Cindy wants two children while Desmond does not believe in the use of contraceptive and wants eight children. He bases his argument on Genesis 1:28 where God commanded the man and woman to be fruitful and multiply. Desmond and Cindy are coming to you for help. What will you say to them?

(Use scripture references to support your responses)

Scenario Two:

Suppose you have two teenage daughters who are active in church. One day you happen to hear the older one telling the younger that she is contemplating getting into a relationship with a young man from a congregation that embraces a doctrine contrary to the one you raised your daughter to embrace. How would you approach this situation? How would you advice her based on the Bible?

Scenario Three:

"She is not the same beautiful woman I married. She has gotten so fat and she is always tired" Jeff regurgitated his feelings to the pastor as Daisy sat silently staring at the purse in her lap. Jeff had asked her for a divorce claiming that he was no longer in love with her. When their pastor had asked their reason for getting married, Jeff quickly stated that they were in love and she made him feel like no other woman did. If you were their pastor, how would you counsel this couple?

Scenario Four:

Susan and Nicholas are both leaders in their local church. They have been married for five years but in the last two years she has noticed that he is very short tempered. Whenever they had a disagreement, he would display fits of rage: yelling at her, throwing items and slamming his hands into the walls and tables. However, he has never hit her. She is concerned and would like to know if the man she has known all these years is an abuser and wants to know what she should do?

Scenario Five:

As a child, Jonathan would helplessly stand by and watch his father physically abuse his mother. He hated his father and as he grew older and stronger, he started to stand against him every time he was about to hit her. Jonathan vowed to himself that he would never hit a woman until recently when he and his wife got into a heated argument. He could not explain what had happened but before he could stop himself, he had slapped her across the face.

Now he is withdrawn and distraught by his action with this hunting questing in his mind: "am I turning into my father?"

Discuss this case. How would you counsel Jonathan?

Scenario Six:

Matt 18:21-22 AMP

> *21 Then Peter came up to Him and said, Lord, how many times may my brother sin against me and I forgive him and let it go? [As many as] up to seven times?*
>
> *22 Jesus answered him, I tell you, not up to seven times, but seventy times seven!*

Rex and Jim have been best friends since grade school and although they are now adults with families of their own, they are inseparable. Rex has found out after having suspected that Jim and his wife have been having an affair for approximately one year. They have both apologized and begged his forgiveness. He has decided to forgive them. However, he does not want Jim to visit his home any longer. Has Rex truly forgiven Jim? Discuss using scriptural references where applicable.

ENDNOTES

i   http://en.wikipedia.org/wiki/Divorce

ii   http://www.biblestudytools.com/dictionaries/bakers-evangelical-dictionary/divorce.html

iii   http://www.biblestudytools.com/dictionaries/bakers-evangelical-dictionary/divorce.html

iv   Many of the fact stated in the two section: Divorce in the Old Testament and Divorce in the New Testament were taken from http://www.biblestudytools.com/dictionaries/bakers-evangelical-dictionary/divorce.html

v   Thayer and Smith. *"Greek Lexicon entry for Porneia"*. "The KJV New Testament Greek Lexicon".

vi

vii   *"How to recognize abuse and the people who are abusers"*, modified Tuesday, July 24, 2007, http://www.ilrctbay.com/upload/custom/abuse/content/abusers.htm

viii   Many of the Characteristics mentioned here were taken from: Hidden Hurt *"Abuse Victim Characteristics"* Copyright© 2002 - 2012 Hidden Hurt, http://www.hiddenhurt.co.uk/abuse_victim_characteristics.html

Some Scripture references were taken from:

- GOD'S WORD Copyright © 1995 by God's Word to the Nations Bible Society. All rights reserved.)
- THE MESSAGE: The Bible in Contemporary Language © 2002 by Eugene H. Peterson. All rights reserved.

Others were taken from:

- The New King James Version
- the Amplified Version
- The New International Version
- King James Version

The Hebrew and Greek Definitions were taken from:

- Biblesoft's New Exhaustive Strong's Numbers and Concordance with Expanded Greek-Hebrew Dictionary. Copyright © 1994, 2003, 2006 Biblesoft, Inc. and International Bible Translators, Inc.)
- McClintock and Strong Encyclopedia, Electronic Database. Copyright © 2000, 2003, 2005, 2006 by Biblesoft, Inc